CLEP-18   COLLEGE-LEVEL EXAMINATION
          PROGRAM SERIES

This is your
PASSBOOK for...

Introduction to Business Management

Test Preparation Study Guide
Questions & Answers

NATIONAL LEARNING CORPORATION®

COPYRIGHT NOTICE

This book is SOLELY intended for, is sold ONLY to, and its use is RESTRICTED to individual, bona fide applicants or candidates who qualify by virtue of having seriously filed applications for appropriate license, certificate, professional and/or promotional advancement, higher school matriculation, scholarship, or other legitimate requirements of education and/or governmental authorities.

This book is NOT intended for use, class instruction, tutoring, training, duplication, copying, reprinting, excerption, or adaptation, etc., by:

1) Other publishers
2) Proprietors and/or Instructors of "Coaching" and/or Preparatory Courses
3) Personnel and/or Training Divisions of commercial, industrial, and governmental organizations
4) Schools, colleges, or universities and/or their departments and staffs, including teachers and other personnel
5) Testing Agencies or Bureaus
6) Study groups which seek by the purchase of a single volume to copy and/or duplicate and/or adapt this material for use by the group as a whole without having purchased individual volumes for each of the members of the group
7) Et al.

Such persons would be in violation of appropriate Federal and State statutes.

PROVISION OF LICENSING AGREEMENTS – Recognized educational, commercial, industrial, and governmental institutions and organizations, and others legitimately engaged in educational pursuits, including training, testing, and measurement activities, may address request for a licensing agreement to the copyright owners, who will determine whether, and under what conditions, including fees and charges, the materials in this book may be used them. In other words, a licensing facility exists for the legitimate use of the material in this book on other than an individual basis. However, it is asseverated and affirmed here that the material in this book CANNOT be used without the receipt of the express permission of such a licensing agreement from the Publishers. Inquiries re licensing should be addressed to the company, attention rights and permissions department.

All rights reserved, including the right of reproduction in whole or in part, in any form or by any means, electronic or mechanical, including photocopying, recording, or by any information storage and retrieval system, without permission in writing from the Publisher.

Copyright © 2025 by
National Learning Corporation

212 Michael Drive, Syosset, NY 11791
(516) 921-8888 • www.passbooks.com
E-mail: info@passbooks.com

PASSBOOK® SERIES

THE *PASSBOOK® SERIES* has been created to prepare applicants and candidates for the ultimate academic battlefield – the examination room.

At some time in our lives, each and every one of us may be required to take an examination – for validation, matriculation, admission, qualification, registration, certification, or licensure.

Based on the assumption that every applicant or candidate has met the basic formal educational standards, has taken the required number of courses, and read the necessary texts, the *PASSBOOK® SERIES* furnishes the one special preparation which may assure passing with confidence, instead of failing with insecurity. Examination questions – together with answers – are furnished as the basic vehicle for study so that the mysteries of the examination and its compounding difficulties may be eliminated or diminished by a sure method.

This book is meant to help you pass your examination provided that you qualify and are serious in your objective.

The entire field is reviewed through the huge store of content information which is succinctly presented through a provocative and challenging approach – the question-and-answer method.

A climate of success is established by furnishing the correct answers at the end of each test.

You soon learn to recognize types of questions, forms of questions, and patterns of questioning. You may even begin to anticipate expected outcomes.

You perceive that many questions are repeated or adapted so that you can gain acute insights, which may enable you to score many sure points.

You learn how to confront new questions, or types of questions, and to attack them confidently and work out the correct answers.

You note objectives and emphases, and recognize pitfalls and dangers, so that you may make positive educational adjustments.

Moreover, you are kept fully informed in relation to new concepts, methods, practices, and directions in the field.

You discover that you are actually taking the examination all the time: you are preparing for the examination by "taking" an examination, not by reading extraneous and/or supererogatory textbooks.

In short, this PASSBOOK®, used directedly, should be an important factor in helping you to pass your test.

NONTRADITIONAL EDUCATION

Students returning to school as adults bring more varied experience to their studies than do the teenagers who begin college shortly after graduating from high school. As a result, there are numerous programs for students with nontraditional learning curves. Hundreds of colleges and universities grant degrees to people who cannot attend classes at a regular campus or have already learned what the college is supposed to teach.

You can earn nontraditional education credits in many ways:
- Passing standardized exams
- Demonstrating knowledge gained through experience
- Completing campus-based coursework, and
- Taking courses off campus

Some methods of assessing learning for credit are objective, such as standardized tests. Others are more subjective, such as a review of life experiences.

With some help from four hypothetical characters – Alice, Vin, Lynette, and Jorge – this article describes nontraditional ways of earning educational credit. It begins by describing programs in which you can earn a high school diploma without spending 4 years in a classroom. The college picture is more complicated, so it is presented in two parts: one on gaining credit for what you know through course work or experience, and a second on college degree programs. The final section lists resources for locating more information.

Earning High School Credit

People who were prevented from finishing high school as teenagers have several options if they want to do so as adults. Some major cities have back-to-school programs that allow adults to attend high school classes with current students. But the more practical alternatives for most adults are to take the General Educational Development (GED) tests or to earn a high school diploma by demonstrating their skills or taking correspondence classes.

Of course, these options do not match the experience of staying in high school and graduating with one's friends. But they are viable alternatives for adult learners committed to meeting and, often, continuing their educational goals.

GED Program

Alice quit high school her sophomore year and took a job to help support herself, her younger brother, and their newly widowed mother. Now an adult, she wants to earn her high school diploma – and then go on to college. Because her job as head cook and her family responsibilities keep her busy during the day, she plans to get a high school equivalency diploma. She will study for, and take, the GED tests. Every year, about half a million adults earn their high school credentials this way. A GED diploma is accepted in lieu of a high school one by more than 90 percent of employers, colleges, and universities, so it is a good choice for someone like Alice.

The GED testing program is sponsored by the American Council on Education and State and local education departments. It consists of examinations in five subject areas: Writing, science, mathematics, social studies, and literature and the arts. The tests also measure skills such as analytical ability, problem solving, reading comprehension, and ability to understand and apply information. Most of the questions are multiple choice; the writing test includes an essay section on a topic of general interest.

Eligibility rules for taking the exams vary, but some states require that you must be at least 18. Tests are given in English, Spanish, and French. In addition to standard print, versions in large print, Braille, and audiocassette are also available. Total time allotted for the tests is 7 1/2 hours.

The GED tests are not easy. About one-fourth of those who complete the exams every year do not pass. Passing scores are established by administering the tests to a sample of graduating high school seniors. The minimum standard score is set so that about one-third of graduating seniors would not pass the tests if they took them.

Because of the difficulty of the tests, people need to prepare themselves to take them. Often, they start by taking the Official GED Practice Tests, usually available through a local adult education center. Centers are listed in your phone book's blue pages under "Adult Education," "Continuing Education," or "GED." Adult education centers also have information about GED preparation classes and self-study materials. Classes are generally arranged to accommodate adults' work schedules. National Learning Corporation publishes several study guides that aim to thoroughly prepare test-takers for the GED.

School districts, colleges, adult education centers, and community organizations have information about GED testing schedules and practice tests. For more information, contact them, your nearest GED testing center, or:

GED Testing Service
One Dupont Circle, NW, Suite 250
Washington, DC 20036-1163
1(800) 62-MY GED (626-9433)
(202) 939-9490

Skills Demonstration

Adults who have acquired high school level skills through experience might be eligible for the National External Diploma Program. This alternative to the GED does not involve any direct instruction. Instead, adults seeking a high school diploma must demonstrate mastery of 65 competencies in 8 general areas: Communication; computation; occupational preparedness; and self, social, consumer, scientific, and technological awareness.

Mastery is shown through the completion of the tasks. For example, a participant could prove competency in computation by measuring a room for carpeting, figuring out the amount of carpet needed, and computing the cost.

Before being accepted for the program, adults undergo an evaluation. Tests taken at one of the program's offices measure reading, writing, and mathematics abilities. A take-home segment includes a self-assessment of current skills, an individual skill evaluation, and an occupational interest and aptitude test.

Adults accepted for the program have weekly meetings with an assessor. At the meeting, the assessor reviews the participant's work from the previous week. If the task has not been completed properly, the assessor explains the mistake. Participants continue to correct their errors until they master each competency. A high school diploma is awarded upon proven mastery of all 65 competencies.

Fourteen States and the District of Columbia now offer the External Diploma Program. For more information, contact:

External Diploma Program
One Dupont Circle, NW, Suite 250
Washington, DC 20036-1193
(202) 939-9475

Correspondence and Distance Study

Vin dropped out of high school during his junior year because his family's frequent moves made it difficult for him to continue his studies. He promised himself at the time he dropped out that he would someday finish the courses needed for his diploma. For people like Vin, who prefer to earn a traditional diploma in a nontraditional way, there are about a dozen accredited courses of study for earning a high school diploma by correspondence, or distance study. The programs are either privately run, affiliated with a university, or administered by a State education department.

Distance study diploma programs have no residency requirements, allowing students to continue their studies from almost any location. Depending on the course of study, students need not be enrolled full time and usually have more flexible schedules for finishing their work. Selection of courses ranges from vo-tech to college prep, and some programs place different emphasis on the types of diplomas offered. University affiliated schools, for example, allow qualified students to take college courses along with their high school ones. Students can then apply the college credits toward a degree at that university or transfer them to another institution.

Taking courses by distance study is often more challenging and time consuming than attending classes, especially for adults who have other obligations. Success depends on each student's motivation. Students usually do reading assignments on their own. Written exercises, which they complete and send to an instructor for grading, supplement their reading material.

A list of some accredited high schools that offer diplomas by distance study is available free from the Distance Education and Training Council, formerly known as the National Home Study Council. Request the "DETC Directory of Accredited Institutions" from:

The Distance Education and Training Council
1601 18th Street, NW.
Washington, DC 20009-2529
(202) 234-5100

Some publications profiling nontraditional college programs include addresses and descriptions of several high school correspondence ones. See the Resources section at the end of this article for more information.

Getting College Credit For What You Know

Adults can receive college credit for prior coursework, by passing examinations, and documenting experiential learning. With help from a college advisor, nontraditional students should assess their skills, establish their educational goals, and determine the number of college credits they might be eligible for.

Even before you meet with a college advisor, you should collect all your school and training records. Then, make a list of all knowledge and abilities acquired through experience, no matter how irrelevant they seem to your chosen field. Next, determine your educational goals: What specific field do you wish to study? What kind of a degree do you want? Finally, determine how your past work fits into the field of study. Later on, you will evaluate educational programs to find one that's right for you.

People who have complex educational or experiential learning histories might want to have their learning evaluated by the Regents Credit Bank. The Credit Bank, operated by Regents College of the University of the State of New York, allows people to consolidate credits earned through college, experience, or other methods. Special assessments are available for Regents College enrollees whose knowledge in a specific field cannot be adequately evaluated by standardized exams. For more information, contact the Regents Credit Bank at:

Regents College
7 Columbia Circle
Albany, NY 12203-5159
(518) 464-8500

Credit For Prior College Coursework

When Lynette was in college during the 1970s, she attended several different schools and took a variety of courses. She did well in some classes and poorly in others. Now that she is a successful business owner and has more focus, Lynette thinks she should forget about her previous coursework and start from scratch. Instead, she should start from where she is.

Lynette should have all her transcripts sent to the colleges or universities of her choice and let an admissions officer determine which classes are applicable toward a degree. A few credits here and there may not seem like much, but they add up. Even if the subjects do not seem relevant to any major, they might be counted as elective credits toward a degree. And comparing the cost of transcripts with the cost of college courses, it makes sense to spend a few dollars per transcript for a chance to save hundreds, and perhaps thousands, of dollars in books and tuition.

Rules for transferring credits apply to all prior coursework at accredited colleges and universities, whether done on campus or off. Courses completed off campus, often called extended learning, include those available to students through independent study and correspondence. Many schools have extended learning programs; Brigham Young University, for example, offers more than 300 courses through its Department of Independent Study. One type of extended learning is distance learning, a form of correspondence study by technological means such as television, video and audio, CD-ROM, electronic mail, and computer tutorials. See the Resources section at the end of this article for more information about publications available from the National University Continuing Education Association.

Any previously earned college credits should be considered for transfer, no matter what the subject or the grade received. Many schools do not accept the transfer of courses graded below a C or ones taken more than a designated number of years ago. Some colleges and universities also have limits on the number of credits that can be transferred and applied toward a degree. But not all do. For example, Thomas Edison State College, New Jersey's State college for adults, accepts the transfer of all 120 hours of credit required for a baccalaureate degree – provided all the credits are transferred from regionally accredited schools, no more than 80 are at the junior college level, and the student's grades overall and in the field of study average out to C.

To assign credit for prior coursework, most schools require original transcripts. This means you must complete a form or send a written, signed request to have your transcripts released directly to a college or university. Once you have chosen the schools you want to apply to, contact the schools you attended before. Find out how much each transcript costs, and ask them to send your transcripts to the ones you are applying to. Write a letter that includes your name (and names used during attendance, if different) and dates of attendance, along with the names and addresses of the schools to which your transcripts should be sent. Include payment and mail to the registrar at the schools you have attended. The registrar's office will process your request and send an official transcript of your coursework to the colleges or universities you have designated.

Credit For Noncollege Courses

Colleges and universities are not the only ones that offer classes. Volunteer organizations and employers often provide formal training worth college credit. The American Council on Education has two programs that assess thousands of specific courses and make recommendations on the amount of college credit they are worth. Colleges and universities accept the recommendations or use them as guidelines.

One program evaluates educational courses sponsored by government agencies, business and industry, labor unions, and professional and voluntary organizations. It is the Program on Noncollegiate Sponsored Instruction (PONSI). Some of the training seminars Alice has participated in covered topics such as food preparation, kitchen safety, and nutrition. Although she has not yet earned her GED, Alice can earn college credit because of her completion of these formal job-training seminars. The number of credits each seminar is worth does not hinge on Alice's current eligibility for college enrollment.

The other program evaluates courses offered by the Army, Navy, Air Force, Marines, Coast Guard, and Department of Defense. It is the Military Evaluations Program. Jorge has never attended college, but the engineering technology classes he completed as part of his military training are worth college credit. And as an Army veteran, Jorge is eligible for a service that takes the evaluations one step further. The Army/American Council on Education Registry Transcript System (AARTS) will provide Jorge with an individualized transcript of American Council on Education credit recommendations for all courses he completed, the military occupational specialties (MOS's) he held, and examinations he passed while in the Army. All Army and National Guard enlisted personnel and veterans who enlisted after October 1981 are eligible for the transcript. Similar services are being considered by the Navy and Marine Corps.

To obtain a free transcript, see your Army Education Center for a 5454R transcript request form. Include your name, Social Security number, basic active service date, and complete address where you want the transcript sent. Mail your request to:
AARTS Operations Center
415 McPherson Ave.
Fort Leavenworth, KS 66027-1373

Recommendations for PONSI are published in *The National Guide to Educational Credit for Training Programs*; military program recommendations are in *The Guide to the Evaluation of Educational Experiences in the Armed Forces*. See the Resources section at the end of this article for more information about these publications.

Former military personnel who took a foreign language course through the Defense Language Institute may request course transcripts by sending their name, Social Security number, course title, duration of the course, and graduation date to:

Commandant, Defense Language Institute
Attn: ATFL-DAA-AR
Transcripts
Presidio of Monterey
Monterey, CA 93944-5006

Not all of Jorge's and Alice's courses have been assessed by the American Council on Education. Training courses that have no Council credit recommendation should still be assessed by an advisor at the schools they want to attend. Course descriptions, class notes, test scores, and other documentation may be helpful for comparing training courses to their college equivalents. An oral examination or other demonstration of competency might also be required.

There is no guarantee you will receive all the credits you are seeking – but you certainly won't if you make no attempt.

Credit By Examination

Standardized tests are the best-known method of receiving college credit without taking courses. These exams are often taken by high school students seeking advanced placement for college, but they are also available to adult learners. Testing programs and colleges and universities offer exams in a number of subjects. Two U.S. Government institutes have foreign language exams for employees that also may be worth college credit.

It is important to understand that receiving a passing score on these exams does not mean you get college credit automatically. Each school determines which test results it will accept, minimum scores required, how scores are converted for credit, and the amount of credit, if any, to be assigned. Most colleges and universities accept the American Council on Education credit recommendations, published every other year in the 250-page *Guide to Educational Credit by Examination*. For more information, contact:

The American Council on Education
Credit by Examination Program
One Dupont Circle, Suite 250
Washington, DC 20036-1193
(202) 939-9434

Testing programs:

You might know some of the five national testing programs by their acronyms or initials: CLEP, ACT PEP: RCE, DANTES, AP, and NOCTI. (The meanings of these initialisms are explained below.) There is some overlap among programs; for example, four of them have introductory accounting exams. Since you will not be awarded credit more than once for a specific subject, you should carefully evaluate each program for the subject exams you wish to take. And before taking an exam, make sure you will be awarded credit by the college or university you plan to attend.

CLEP (College-Level Examination Program), administered by the College Board, is the most widely accepted of the national testing programs; more than 2,800 accredited schools award credit for passing exam scores. Each test covers material taught in basic undergraduate courses. There are five general exams – English composition, humanities, college mathematics, natural sciences, and social sciences and history – and many subject exams. Most exams are entirely multiple-choice, but English composition exams may include an essay section. For more information, contact:

>CLEP
>P.O. Box 6600
>Princeton, NJ 08541-6600
>(609) 771-7865

ACT PEP: RCE (American College Testing Proficiency Exam Program: Regents College Examinations) tests are given in 38 subjects within arts and sciences, business, education, and nursing. Each exam is recommended for either lower- or upper-level credit. Exams contain either objective or extended response questions, and are graded according to a standard score, letter grade, or pass/fail. Fees vary, depending on the subject and type of exam. For more information or to request free study guides, contact:

>ACT PEP: Regents College Examinations
>P.O. Box 4014
>Iowa City, IA 52243
>(319) 337-1387
>(New York State residents must contact Regents College directly.)

DANTES (Defense Activity for Nontraditional Education Support) standardized tests are developed by the Educational Testing Service for the Department of Defense. Originally administered only to military personnel, the exams have been available to the public since 1983. About 50 subject tests cover business, mathematics, social science, physical science, humanities, foreign languages, and applied technology. Most of the tests consist entirely of multiple-choice questions. Schools determine their own administering fees and testing schedules. For more information or to request free study sheets, contact:

>DANTES Program Office
>Mail Stop 31-X
>Educational Testing Service
>Princeton, NJ 08541
>1(800) 257-9484

The AP (Advanced Placement) Program is a cooperative effort between secondary schools and colleges and universities. AP exams are developed each year by committees of college and high school faculty appointed by the College Board and assisted by consultants from the Educational Testing Service. Subjects include arts and languages, natural sciences, computer science, social sciences, history, and mathematics. Most tests are 2 or 3 hours long and include both multiple-choice and essay questions. AP courses are available to help students prepare for exams, which are offered in the spring. For more information about the Advanced Placement Program, contact:

>Advanced Placement Services
>P.O. Box 6671
>Princeton, NJ 08541-6671
>(609) 771-7300

NOCTI (National Occupational Competency Testing Institute) assessments are designed for people like Alice, who have vocational-technical skills that cannot be evaluated by other tests. NOCTI assesses competency at two levels: Student/job ready and teacher/experienced worker. Standardized evaluations are available for occupations such as auto-body repair, electronics, mechanical drafting, quantity food preparation, and upholstering. The tests consist of multiple-choice questions and a performance component. Other services include workshops, customized assessments, and pre-testing. For more information, contact:

NOCTI
500 N. Bronson Ave.
Ferris State University
Big Rapids, MI 49307
(616) 796-4699

Colleges and universities:

Many colleges and universities have credit-by-exam programs, through which students earn credit by passing a comprehensive exam for a course offered by the institution. Among the most widely recognized are the programs at Ohio University, the University of North Carolina, Thomas Edison State College, and New York University.

Ohio University offers about 150 examinations for credit. In addition, you may sometimes arrange to take special examinations in non-laboratory courses offered at Ohio University. To take a test for credit, you must enroll in the course. If you plan to transfer the credit earned, you also need written permission from an official at your school. Books and study materials are available, for a cost, through the university. Exams must be taken within 6 months of the enrollment date; most last 3 hours. You may arrange to take the exam off campus if you do not live near the university.

Ohio University is on the quarter-hour system; most courses are worth 4 quarter hours, the equivalent of 3 semester hours. For more information, contact:

Independent Study
Tupper Hall 302
Ohio University
Athens, OH 45701-2979
1(800) 444-2910
(614) 593-2910

The University of North Carolina offers a credit-by-examination option for 140 independent study (correspondence) courses in foreign languages, humanities, social sciences, mathematics, business administration, education, electrical and computer engineering, health administration, and natural sciences. To take an exam, you must request and receive approval from both the course instructor and the independent studies department. Exams must be taken within six months of enrollment, and you may register for no more than two at a time. If you are not near the University's Chapel Hill campus, you may take your exam under supervision at an accredited college, university, community college, or technical institute. For more information, contact:

Independent Studies
CB #1020, The Friday Center
UNC-Chapel Hill
Chapel Hill, NC 27599-1020
1(800) 862-5669 / (919) 962-1134

The Thomas Edison College Examination Program offers more than 50 exams in liberal arts, business, and professional areas. Thomas Edison State College administers tests twice a month in Trenton, New Jersey; however, students may arrange to take their tests with a proctor at any accredited American college or university or U.S. military base. Most of the tests are multiple choice; some also include short answer or essay questions. Time limits range from 90 minutes to 4 hours, depending on the exam. For more information, contact:

Thomas Edison State College
TECEP, Office of Testing and Assessment
101 W. State Street
Trenton, NJ 08608-1176
(609) 633-2844

New York University's Foreign Language Program offers proficiency exams in more than 40 languages, from Albanian to Yiddish. Two exams are available in each language: The 12-point test is equivalent to 4 undergraduate semesters, and the 16-point exam may lead to upper level credit. The tests are given at the university's Foreign Language Department throughout the year.

Proof of foreign language proficiency does not guarantee college credit. Some colleges and universities accept transcripts only for languages commonly taught, such as French and Spanish. Nontraditional programs are more likely than traditional ones to grant credit for proficiency in other languages.

For an informational brochure and registration form for NYU's foreign language proficiency exams, contact:

New York University
Foreign Language Department
48 Cooper Square, Room 107
New York, NY 10003
(212) 998-7030

Government institutes:

The Defense Language Institute and Foreign Service Institute administer foreign language proficiency exams for personnel stationed abroad. Usually, the tests are given at the end of intensive language courses or upon completion of service overseas. But some people – like Jorge, who knows Spanish – speak another language fluently and may be allowed to take a proficiency exam in that language before completing their tour of duty. Contact one of the offices listed below to obtain transcripts of those scores. Proof of proficiency does not guarantee college credit, however, as discussed above.

To request score reports from the Defense Language Institute for Defense Language Proficiency Tests, send your name, Social Security number, language for which you were tested, and, most importantly, when and where you took the exam to:

Commandant, Defense Language Institute
Attn: ATFL-ES-T
DLPT Score Report Request
Presidio of Monterey
Monterey, CA 93944-5006

To request transcripts of scores for Foreign Service Institute exams, send your name, Social Security number, language for which you were tested, and dates or year of exams to:

Foreign Service Institute
Arlington Hall
4020 Arlington Boulevard
Rosslyn, VA 22204-1500
Attn: Testing Office (Send your request to the attention of the testing office of the foreign language in which you were tested)

Credit For Experience

Experiential learning credit may be given for knowledge gained through job responsibilities, personal hobbies, volunteer opportunities, homemaking, and other experiences. Colleges and universities base credit awards on the knowledge you have attained, not for the experience alone. In addition, the knowledge must be college level; not just any learning will do. Throwing horseshoes as a hobby is not likely to be worth college credit. But if you've done research on how and where the sport originated, visited blacksmiths, organized tournaments, and written a column for a trade journal — well, that's a horseshoe of a different color.

Adults attempting to get credit for their experience should be forewarned: Having your experience evaluated for college credit is time-consuming, tedious work — not an easy shortcut for people who want quick-fix college credits. And not all experience, no matter how valuable, is the equivalent of college courses.

Requesting college credit for your experiential learning can be tricky. You should get assistance from a credit evaluations officer at the school you plan to attend, but you should also have a general idea of what your knowledge is worth. A common method for converting knowledge into credit is to use a college catalog. Find course titles and descriptions that match what you have learned through experience, and request the number of credits offered for those courses.

Once you know what credit to ask for, you must usually present your case in writing to officials at the college you plan to attend. The most common form of presenting experiential learning for credit is the portfolio. A portfolio is a written record of your knowledge along with a request for equivalent college credit. It includes an identification and description of the knowledge for which you are requesting credit, an explanatory essay of how the knowledge was gained and how it fits into your educational plans, documentation that you have acquired such knowledge, and a request for college credit. Required elements of a portfolio vary by schools but generally follow those guidelines.

In identifying knowledge you have gained, be specific about exactly what you have learned. For example, it is not enough for Lynette to say she runs a business. She must identify the knowledge she has gained from running it, such as personnel management, tax law, marketing strategy, and inventory review. She must also include brief descriptions about her knowledge of each to support her claims of having those skills.

The essay gives you a chance to relay something about who you are. It should address your educational goals, include relevant autobiographical details, and be well organized, neat, and convey confidence. In his essay, Jorge might first state his goal of becoming an engineer. Then he would explain why he joined the Army, where he got hands-on training and experience in developing and servicing electronic equipment.

This, he would say, led to his hobby of creating remote-controlled model cars, of which he has built 20. His conclusion would highlight his accomplishments and tie them to his desire to become an electronic engineer.

Documentation is evidence that you've learned what you claim to have learned. You can show proof of knowledge in a variety of ways, including audio or video recordings, letters from current or former employers describing your specific duties and job performance, blueprints, photographs or artwork, and transcripts of certifying exams for professional licenses and certification – such as Alice's certification from the American Culinary Federation. Although documentation can take many forms, written proof alone is not always enough. If it is impossible to document your knowledge in writing, find out if your experiential learning can be assessed through supplemental oral exams by a faculty expert.

Earning a College Degree

Nontraditional students often have work, family, and financial obligations that prevent them from quitting their jobs to attend school full time. Can they still meet their educational goals? Yes.

More than 150 accredited colleges and universities have nontraditional bachelor's degree programs that require students to spend little or no time on campus; over 300 others have nontraditional campus-based degree programs. Some of those schools, as well as most junior and community colleges, offer associate's degrees nontraditionally. Each school with a nontraditional course of study determines its own rules for awarding credit for prior coursework, exams, or experience, as discussed previously. Most have charges on top of tuition for providing these special services.

Several publications profile nontraditional degree programs; see the Resources section at the end of this article for more information. To determine which school best fits your academic profile and educational goals, first list your criteria. Then, evaluate nontraditional programs based on their accreditation, features, residency requirements, and expenses. Once you have chosen several schools to explore further, write to them for more information. Detailed explanations of school policies should help you decide which ones you want to apply to.

Get beyond the printed word – especially the glowing words each school writes about itself. Check out the schools you are considering with higher education authorities, alumni, employers, family members, and friends. If possible, visit the campus to talk to students and instructors and sit in on a few classes, even if you will be completing most or all of your work off campus. Ask school officials questions about such things as enrollment numbers, graduation rate, faculty qualifications, and confusing details about the application process or academic policies. After you have thoroughly investigated each prospective college or university, you can make an informed decision about which is right for you.

Accreditation

Accreditation is a process colleges and universities submit to voluntarily for getting their credentials. An accredited school has been investigated and visited by teams of observers and has periodic inspections by a private accrediting agency. The initial review can take two years or more.

Regional agencies accredit entire schools, and professional agencies accredit either specialized schools or departments within schools. Although there are no national accrediting standards, not just any accreditation will do. Countless "accreditation associations" have been invented by schools, many of which have no academic programs and sell phony degrees, to accredit themselves. But 6 regional and about 80 professional accrediting associations in the United States are recognized by the U.S. Department of Education or the Commission on Recognition of Postsecondary Accreditation. When checking accreditation, these are the names to look for. For more information about accreditation and accrediting agencies, contact:

Institutional Participation Oversight Service Accreditation and State Liaison Division
U.S. Department of Education
ROB 3, Room 3915
600 Independence Ave., SW
Washington, DC 20202-5244
(202) 708-7417

Because accreditation is not mandatory, lack of accreditation does not necessarily mean a school or program is bad. Some schools choose not to apply for accreditation, are in the process of applying, or have educational methods too unconventional for an accrediting association's standards. For the nontraditional student, however, earning a degree from a college or university with recognized accreditation is an especially important consideration. Although nontraditional education is becoming more widely accepted, it is not yet mainstream. Employers skeptical of a degree earned in a nontraditional manner are likely to be even less accepting of one from an unaccredited school.

Program Features

Because nontraditional students have diverse educational objectives, nontraditional schools are diverse in what they offer. Some programs are geared toward helping students organize their scattered educational credits to get a degree as quickly as possible. Others cater to those who may have specific credits or experience but need assistance in completing requirements. Whatever your educational profile, you should look for a program that works with you in obtaining your educational goals.

A few nontraditional programs have special admissions policies for adult learners like Alice, who plan to earn their GEDs but want to enroll in college in the meantime. Other features of nontraditional programs include individualized learning agreements, intensive academic counseling, cooperative learning and internship placement, and waiver of some prerequisites or other requirements – as well as college credit for prior coursework, examinations, and experiential learning, all discussed previously.

Lynette, whose primary goal is to finish her degree, wants to earn maximum credits for her business experience. She will look for programs that do not limit the number of credits awarded for equivalency exams and experiential learning. And since well-documented proof of knowledge is essential for earning experiential learning credits, Lynette should make sure the program she chooses provides assistance to students submitting a portfolio.

Jorge, on the other hand, has more credits than he needs in certain areas and is willing to forego some. To become an engineer, he must have a bachelor's degree; but because he is accustomed to hands-on learning, Jorge is interested in getting experience as he gains more technical skills. He will concentrate on finding schools with strong cooperative education, supervised fieldwork, or internship programs.

Residency Requirements

Programs are sometimes deemed nontraditional because of their residency requirements. Many people think of residency for colleges and universities in terms of tuition, with in-state students paying less than out-of-state ones. Residency also may refer to where a student lives, either on or off campus, while attending school.

But in nontraditional education, residency usually refers to how much time students must spend on campus, regardless of whether they attend classes there. In some nontraditional programs, students need not ever step foot on campus. Others require only a very short residency, such as one day or a few weeks. Many schools have standard residency requirements of several semesters but schedule classes for evenings or weekends to accommodate working adults.

Lynette, who previously took courses by independent study, prefers to earn credits by distance study. She will focus on schools that have no residency requirement. Several colleges and universities have nonresident degree completion programs for adults with some college credit. Under the direction of a faculty advisor, students devise a plan for earning their remaining credits. Methods for earning credits include independent study, distance learning, seminars, supervised fieldwork, and group study at arranged sites. Students may have to earn a certain number of credits through the degree-granting institution. But many programs allow students to take courses at accredited schools of their choice for transfer toward their degree.

Alice wants to attend lectures but has an unpredictable schedule. Her best course of action will be to seek out short residency programs that require students to attend seminars once or twice a semester. She can take courses that are televised and videotape them to watch when her schedule permits, with the seminars helping to ensure that she properly completes her coursework. Many colleges and universities with short residency requirements also permit students to earn some credits elsewhere, by whatever means the student chooses.

Some fields of study require classroom instruction. As Jorge will discover, few colleges and universities allow students to earn a bachelor's degree in engineering entirely through independent study. Nontraditional residency programs are designed to accommodate adults' daytime work schedules. Jorge should look for programs offering evening, weekend, summer, and accelerated courses.

Tuition and Other Expenses

The final decisions about which schools Alice, Jorge, and Lynette attend may hinge in large part on a single issue: Cost. And rising tuition is only part of the equation. Beginning with application fees and continuing through graduation fees, college expenses add up.

Traditional and nontraditional students have some expenses in common, such as the cost of books and other materials. Tuition might even be the same for some courses, especially for colleges and universities offering standard ones at unusual times. But for nontraditional programs, students may also pay fees for services such as credit or transcript review, evaluation, advisement, and portfolio assessment.

Students are also responsible for postage and handling or setup expenses for independent study courses, as well as for all examination and transcript fees for transferring credits. Usually, the more nontraditional the program, the more detailed the fees. Some schools charge a yearly enrollment fee rather than tuition for degree completion candidates who want their files to remain active.

Although tuition and fees might seem expensive, most educators tell you not to let money come between you and your educational goals. Talk to someone in the financial aid department of the school you plan to attend or check your library for publications about financial aid sources. The U.S. Department of Education publishes a guide to Federal aid programs such as Pell Grants, student loans, and work-study. To order the free 74-page booklet, *The Student Guide: Financial Aid from the U.S. Department of Education,* contact:

Federal Student Aid Information Center
P.O. Box 84
Washington, DC 20044
1 (800) 4FED-AID (433-3243)

Resources

Information on how to earn a high school diploma or college degree without following the usual routes is available from several organizations and in numerous publications. Information on nontraditional graduate degree programs, available for master's through doctoral level, though not discussed in this article, can usually be obtained from the same resources that detail bachelor's degree programs.

National Learning Corporation publishes study guides for all of these exams, for both general examinations and tests in specific subject areas. To order study guides, or to browse their catalog featuring more than 5,000 titles, visit NLC online at www.passbooks.com, or contact them by phone at (800) 632-8888.

Organizations

Adult learners should always contact their local school system, community college, or university to learn about programs that are readily available. The following national organizations can also supply information:

American Council on Education
One Dupont Circle
Washington, DC 20036-1193
(202) 939-9300

Within the American Council on Education, the Center for Adult Learning and Educational Credentials administers the National External Diploma Program, the GED Program, the Program on Noncollegiate Sponsored Instruction, the Credit by Examination Program, and the Military Evaluations Program.

College-Level Examination Program (CLEP)

1. WHAT IS CLEP?

CLEP stands for the College-Level Examination Program, sponsored by the College Board. It is a national program of credit-by-examination that offers you the opportunity to obtain recognition for college-level achievement. No matter when, where, or how you have learned – by means of formal or informal study – you can take CLEP tests. If the results are acceptable to your college, you can receive credit.

You may not realize it, but you probably know more than your academic record reveals. Each day you, like most people, have an opportunity to learn. In private industry and business, as well as at all levels of government, learning opportunities continually occur. If you read widely or intensively in a particular field, think about what you read, discuss it with your family and friends, you are learning. Or you may be learning on a more formal basis by taking a correspondence course, a television or radio course, a course recorded on tape or cassettes, a course assembled into programmed tests, or a course taught in your community adult school or high school.

No matter how, where, or when you gained your knowledge, you may have the opportunity to receive academic credit for your achievement that can be counted toward an undergraduate degree. The College-Level Examination Program (CLEP) enables colleges to evaluate your achievement and give you credit. A wide range of college-level examinations are offered by CLEP to anyone who wishes to take them. Scores on the tests are reported to you and, if you wish, to a college, employer, or individual.

2. WHAT ARE THE PURPOSES OF THE COLLEGE-LEVEL EXAMINATION PROGRAM?

The basic purpose of the College-Level Examination Program is to enable individuals who have acquired their education in nontraditional ways to demonstrate their academic achievement. It is also intended for use by those in higher education, business, industry, government, and other fields who need a reliable method of assessing a person's educational level.

Recognizing that the real issue is not how a person has acquired his education but what education he has, the College Level Examination Program has been designed to serve a variety of purposes. The basic purpose, as listed above, is to enable those who have reached the college level of education in nontraditional ways to assess the level of their achievement and to use the test results in seeking college credit or placement.

In addition, scores on the tests can be used to validate educational experience obtained at a nonaccredited institution or through noncredit college courses.

Some colleges and universities may use the tests to measure the level of educational achievement of their students, and for various institutional research purposes.

Other colleges and universities may wish to use the tests in the admission, placement, and guidance of students who wish to transfer from one institution to another.

Businesses, industries, governmental agencies, and professional groups now accept the results of these tests as a basis for advancement, eligibility for further training, or professional or semi-professional certification.

Many people are interested in the examination simply to assess their own educational progress and attainment.

The college, university, business, industry, or government agency that adopts the tests in the College-Level Examination Program makes its own decision about how it will use and interpret the test scores. The College Board will provide the tests, score them, and report the results either to the individuals who took the tests or the college or agency that administered them. It does NOT, and cannot, award college credit, certify college equivalency, or make recommendations regarding the standards these institutions should establish for the use of the test results.

Therefore, if you are taking the tests to secure credit from an institution, you should FIRST ascertain whether the college or agency involved will accept the scores. Each institution determines which CLEP tests it will accept for credit and the amount of credit it will award. If you want to take tests for college credit, first call, write, or visit the college you wish to attend to inquire about its policy on CLEP scores, as well as its other admission requirements.

The services of the program are also available to people who have been requested to take the tests by an employer, a professional licensing agency, a certifying agency, or by other groups that recognize college equivalency on the basis of satisfactory CLEP scores. You may, of course, take the tests SOLELY for your own information. If you do, your scores will be reported only to you.

While neither CLEP nor the College Board can evaluate previous credentials or award college credit, you will receive, with your scores, basic information to help you interpret your performance on the tests you have taken.

3. WHAT ARE THE COLLEGE-LEVEL EXAMINATIONS?

In order to meet different kinds of curricular organization and testing needs at colleges and universities, the College-Level Examination Program offers 35 different subject tests falling under five separate general categories: Composition and Literature, Foreign Languages, History and Social Sciences, Science and Mathematics, and Business.

4. WHAT ARE THE SUBJECT EXAMINATIONS?

The 35 CLEP tests offered by the College Board are listed below:

COMPOSITION AND LITERATURE:
- American Literature
- Analyzing and Interpreting Literature
- English Composition
- English Composition with Essay
- English Literature
- Freshman College Composition
- Humanities

FOREIGN LANGUAGES
- French
- German
- Spanish

HISTORY AND SOCIAL SCIENCES
- American Government
- Introduction to Educational Psychology
- History of the United States I: Early Colonization to 1877
- History of the United States II: 1865 to the Present
- Human Growth and Development
- Principles of Macroeconomics
- Principles of Microeconomics
- Introductory Psychology
- Social Sciences and History
- Introductory Sociology
- Western Civilization I: Ancient Near East to 1648
- Western Civilization II: 1648 to the Present

SCIENCE AND MATHEMATICS
- College Algebra
- College Algebra-Trigonometry
- Biology
- Calculus
- Chemistry
- College Mathematics
- Natural Sciences
- Trigonometry
- Precalculus

BUSINESS
- Financial Accounting
- Introductory Business Law
- Information Systems and Computer Applications
- Principles of Management
- Principles of Marketing

CLEP Examinations cover material taught in courses that most students take as requirements in the first two years of college. A college usually grants the same amount of credit to students earning satisfactory scores on the CLEP examination as it grants to students successfully completing the equivalent course.

Many examinations are designed to correspond to one-semester courses; some, however, correspond to full-year or two-year courses.

Each exam is 90 minutes long and, except for English Composition with Essay, is made up primarily of multiple-choice questions. Some tests have several other types of questions besides multiple choice. To see a more detailed description of a particular CLEP exam, visit www.collegeboard.com/clep.

The English Composition with Essay exam is the only exam that includes a required essay. This essay is scored by college English faculty designated by CLEP and does not require an additional fee. However, other Composition and Literature tests offer optional essays, which some college and universities require and some do not. These essays are graded by faculty at the individual institutions that require them and require an additional $10 fee. Contact the particular institution to ask about essay requirements, and check with your test center for further details.

All 35 CLEP examinations are administered on computer. If you are unfamiliar with taking a test on a computer, consult the CLEP Sampler online at www.collegeboard.com/clep. The Sampler contains the same tutorials as the actual exams and helps familiarize you with navigation and how to answer different types of questions.

Points are not deducted for wrong or skipped answers – you receive one point for every correct answer. Therefore it is best that an answer is supplied for each exam question, whether it is a guess or not. The number of correct answers is then converted to a formula score. This formula, or "scaled," score is determined by a statistical process called *equating*, which adjusts for slight differences in difficulty between test forms and ensures that your score does not depend on the specific test form you took or how well others did on the same form. The scaled scores range from 20 to 80 – this is the number that will appear on your score report.

To ensure that you complete all questions in the time allotted, you would probably be wise to skip the more difficult or perplexing questions and return to them later. Although the multiple-choice items in these tests are carefully designed so as not to be tricky, misleading, or ambiguous, on the other hand, they are not all direct questions of factual information. They attempt, in their way, to elicit a response that indicates your knowledge or lack of knowledge of the material in question or your ability or inability to use or interpret a fact or idea. Thus, you should concentrate on answering the questions as they appear to be without attempting to out-guess the testmakers.

5. WHAT ARE THE FEES?

The fee for all CLEP examinations is $55. Optional essays required by some institutions are an additional $10.

6. WHEN ARE THE TESTS GIVEN?

CLEP tests are administered year-round. Consult the CLEP website (www.collegeboard.com/clep) and individual test centers for specific information.

7. WHERE ARE THE TESTS GIVEN?

More than 1,300 test centers are located on college and university campuses throughout the country, and additional centers are being established to meet increased needs. Any accredited collegiate institution with an explicit and publicly available policy of credit by examination can become a CLEP test center. To obtain a list of these centers, visit the CLEP website at www.collegeboard.com/clep.

8. HOW DO I REGISTER FOR THE COLLEGE-LEVEL EXAMINATION PROGRAM?

Contact an individual test center for information regarding registration, scheduling and fees. Registration/admission forms can also be obtained on the CLEP website.

9. MAY I REPEAT THE COLLEGE-LEVEL EXAMINATIONS?

You may repeat any examination providing at least six months have passed since you were last administered this test. If you repeat a test within a period of time less than six months, your scores will be cancelled and your fees forfeited. To repeat a test, check the appropriate space on the registration form.

10. WHEN MAY I EXPECT MY SCORE REPORTS?

With the exception of the English Composition with Essay exam, you should receive your score report instantly once the test is complete.

11. HOW SHOULD I PREPARE FOR THE COLLEGE-LEVEL EXAMINATIONS?

This book has been specifically designed to prepare candidates for these examinations. It will help you to consider, study, and review important content, principles, practices, procedures, problems, and techniques in the form of varied and concrete applications.

12. QUESTIONS AND ANSWERS APPEARING IN THIS PUBLICATION

The College-Level Examinations are offered by the College Board. Since copies of past examinations have not been made available, we have used equivalent materials, including questions and answers, which are highly recommended by us as an appropriate means of preparing for these examinations.

If you need additional information about CLEP Examinations, visit www.collegeboard.com/clep.

THE COLLEGE-LEVEL EXAMINATION PROGRAM

How The Program Works

CLEP examinations are administered at many colleges and universities across the country, and most institutions award college credit to those who do well on them. The examinations provide people who have acquired knowledge outside the usual educational settings the opportunity to show that they have learned college-level material without taking certain college courses.

The CLEP examinations cover material that is taught in introductory-level courses at many colleges and universities. Faculties at individual colleges review the tests to ensure that they cover the important material taught in their courses. Colleges differ in the examinations they accept; some colleges accept only two or three of the examinations while others accept nearly all of them.

Although CLEP is sponsored by the College Board and the examinations are scored by Educational Testing Service (ETS), neither of these organizations can award college credit. Only accredited colleges may grant credit toward a degree. When you take a CLEP examination, you may request that a copy of your score report be sent to the college you are attending or plan to attend. After evaluating your scores, the college will decide whether or not to award you credit for a certain course or courses, or to exempt you from them. If the college gives you credit, it will record the number of credits on your permanent record, thereby indicating that you have completed work equivalent to a course in that subject. If the college decides to grant exemption without giving you credit for a course, you will be permitted to omit a course that would normally be required of you and to take a course of your choice instead.

What the Examinations Are Like

The examinations consist mostly of multiple-choice questions to be answered within a 90-minute time limit. Additional information about each CLEP examination is given in the examination guide and on the CLEP website.

Where To Take the Examinations

CLEP examinations are administered throughout the year at the test centers of approximately 1,300 colleges and universities. On the CLEP website, you will find a list of institutions that award credit for satisfactory scores on CLEP examinations. Some colleges administer CLEP examinations to their own students only. Other institutions administer the tests to anyone who registers to take them. If your college does not administer the tests, contact the test centers in your area for information about its testing schedule.

Once you have been tested, your score report will be available instantly. CLEP scores are kept on file at ETS for 20 years; and during this period, for a small fee, you may have your transcript sent to another college or to anyone else you specify. (Your scores will never be sent to anyone without your approval.)

APPROACHING A COLLEGE ABOUT CLEP

The following sections provide a step-by-step approach to learning about the CLEP policy at a particular college or university. The person or office that can best assist students desiring CLEP credit may have a different title at each institution, but the following guidelines will lead you to information about CLEP at any institution.

Adults returning to college often benefit from special assistance when they approach a college. Opportunities for adults to return to formal learning in the classroom are now widespread, and colleges and universities have worked hard to make this a smooth process for older students. Many colleges have established special service offices that are staffed with trained professionals who understand the kinds of problems facing adults returning to college. If you think you might benefit from such assistance, be sure to find out whether these services are available at your college.

How to Apply for College Credit

STEP 1. Obtain the General Information Catalog and a copy of the CLEP policy from the colleges you are considering. If you have not yet applied for admission, ask for an admissions application form too.

Information about admissions and CLEP policies can be obtained by contacting college admissions offices or finding admissions information on the school websites. Tell the admissions officer that you are a prospective student and that you are interested in applying for admission and CLEP credit. Ask for a copy of the publication in which the college's complete CLEP policy is explained. Also get the name and the telephone number of the person to contact in case you have further questions about CLEP.

At this step, you may wish to obtain information from external degree colleges. Many adults find that such colleges suit their needs exceptionally well.

STEP 2. If you have not already been admitted to the college you are considering, look at its admission requirements for undergraduate students to see if you can qualify.

This is an important step because if you can't get into college, you can't get college credit for CLEP. Nearly all colleges require students to be admitted and to enroll in one or more courses before granting the students CLEP credit.

Virtually all public community colleges and a number of four-year state colleges have open admission policies for in-state students. This usually means that they admit anyone who has graduated from high school or has earned a high school equivalency diploma.

If you think you do not meet the admission requirements, contact the admissions office for an interview with a counselor. Colleges do sometimes make exceptions, particularly for adult applicants. State why you want the interview and ask what documents you should bring with you or send in advance. (These materials may include a high school transcript, transcript of previous college work, completed application for admission, etc.) Make an extra effort to have all the information requested in time for the interview.

During the interview, relax and be yourself. Be prepared to state honestly why you think you are ready and able to do college work. If you have already taken CLEP examinations and scored high enough to earn credit, you have shown that you are able to do college work. Mention this achievement to the admissions counselor because it may increase your chances of being accepted. If you have not taken a CLEP examination, you can still improve your chances of being accepted by describing how your job training or independent study has helped prepare you for college-level work. Tell the counselor what you have learned from your work and personal experiences.

STEP 3. Evaluate the college's CLEP policy.

Typically, a college lists all its academic policies, including CLEP policies, in its general catalog. You will probably find the CLEP policy statement under a heading such as Credit-by-Examination, Advanced Standing, Advanced Placement, or External Degree Program. These sections can usually be found in the front of the catalog.

Many colleges publish their credit-by-examination policies in a separate brochure, which is distributed through the campus testing office, counseling center, admissions office, or registrar's office. If you find a very general policy statement in the college catalog, seek clarification from one of these offices.

Review the material in the section of this guide entitled Questions to Ask About a College's CLEP Policy. Use these guidelines to evaluate the college's CLEP policy. If you have not yet taken a CLEP examination, this evaluation will help you decide which examinations to take and whether or not to take the free-response or essay portion. Because individual colleges have different CLEP policies, a review of several policies may help you decide which college to attend.

STEP 4. If you have not yet applied for admission, do so early.

Most colleges expect you to apply for admission several months before you enroll, and it is essential that you meet the published application deadlines. It takes time to process your application for admission; and if you have yet to take a CLEP examination, it will be some time before the college receives and reviews your score report. You will probably want to take some, if not all, of the CLEP examinations you are interested in before you enroll so you know which courses you need not register for. In fact, some colleges require that all CLEP scores be submitted before a student registers.

Complete all forms and include all documents requested with your application(s) for admission. Normally, an admissions decision cannot be reached until all documents have been submitted and evaluated. Unless told to do so, do not send your CLEP scores until you have been officially admitted.

STEP 5. Arrange to take CLEP examination(s) or to submit your CLEP score(s).

You may want to wait to take your CLEP examinations until you know definitely which college you will be attending. Then you can make sure you are taking tests your college will accept for credit. You will also be able to request that your scores be sent to the college, free of charge, when you take the tests.

If you have already taken CLEP examinations, but did not have a copy of your score report sent to your college, you may request the College Board to send an official transcript at any time for a small fee. Use the Transcript Request Form that was sent to you with your score report. If you do not have the form, you may find it online at www.collegeboard.com/clep.

Your CLEP scores will be evaluated, probably by someone in the admissions office, and sent to the registrar's office to be posted on your permanent record once you are enrolled. Procedures vary from college to college, but the process usually begins in the admissions office.

STEP 6. Ask to receive a written notice of the credit you receive for your CLEP score(s).

A written notice may save you problems later, when you submit your degree plan or file for graduation. In the event that there is a question about whether or not you earned CLEP credit, you will have an official record of what credit was awarded. You may also need this verification of course credit if you go for academic counseling before the credit is posted on your permanent record.

STEP 7. Before you register for courses, seek academic counseling.

A discussion with your academic advisor can prevent you from taking unnecessary courses and can tell you specifically what your CLEP credit will mean to you. This step may be accomplished at the time you enroll. Most colleges have orientation sessions for new students prior to each enrollment period. During orientation, students are usually assigned an academic advisor who then gives them individual help in developing long-range plans and a course schedule for the next semester. In conjunction with this counseling, you may be asked to take some additional tests so that you can be placed at the proper course level.

External Degree Programs

If you have acquired a considerable amount of college-level knowledge through job experience, reading, or noncredit courses, if you have accumulated college credits at a variety of colleges over a period of years, or if you prefer studying on your own rather than in a classroom setting, you may want to investigate the possibility of enrolling in an external degree program. Many colleges offer external degree programs that allow you to earn a degree by passing examinations (including CLEP), transferring credit from other colleges, and demonstrating in other ways that you have satisfied the educational requirements. No classroom attendance is required, and the programs are open to out-of-state candidates as well as residents. Thomas A. Edison State College in New Jersey and Charter Oaks College in Connecticut are fully accredited independent state colleges; the New York program is part of the state university system and is also fully accredited. If you are interested in exploring an external degree, you can write for more information to:

Charter Oak College
The Exchange, Suite 171
270 Farmington Avenue
Farmington, CT 06032-1909

Regents External Degree Program
Cultural Education Center
Empire State Plaza
Albany, New York 12230

Thomas A. Edison State College
101 West State Street
Trenton, New Jersey 08608

Many other colleges also have external degree or weekend programs. While they often require that a number of courses be taken on campus, the external degree programs tend to be more flexible in transferring credit, granting credit-by-examination, and allowing independent study than other traditional programs. When applying to a college, you may wish to ask whether it has an external degree or weekend program.

Questions to Ask About a College's CLEP Policy

Before taking CLEP examinations for the purpose of earning college credit, try to find the answers to these questions:

1. Which CLEP examinations are accepted by this college?

A college may accept some CLEP examinations for credit and not others - possibly not the one you are considering. The English faculty may decide to grant college English credit based on the CLEP English Composition examination, but not on the Freshman College Composition examination. Or, the mathematics faculty may decide to grant credit based on the College Mathematics to non-mathematics majors only, requiring majors to take an examination in algebra, trigonometry, or calculus to earn credit. For these reasons, it is important that you know the specific CLEP tests for which you can receive credit.

2. Does the college require the optional free-response (essay) section as well as the objective portion of the CLEP examination you are considering?

Knowing the answer to this question ahead of time will permit you to schedule the optional essay examination when you register to take your CLEP examination.

3. Is credit granted for specific courses? If so, which ones?

You are likely to find that credit will be granted for specific courses and the course titles will be designated in the college's CLEP policy. It is not necessary, however, that credit be granted for a specific course in order for you to benefit from your CLEP credit. For instance, at many liberal arts colleges, all students must take certain types of courses; these courses may be labeled the core curriculum, general education requirements, distribution requirements, or liberal arts requirements. The requirements are often expressed in terms of credit hours. For example, all students may be required to take at least six hours of humanities, six hours of English, three hours of mathematics, six hours of natural science, and six hours of social science, with no particular courses in these disciplines specified. In these instances, CLEP credit may be given as 6 hrs. English credit or 3 hrs. Math credit without specifying for which English or mathematics courses credit has been awarded. In order to avoid possible disappointment, you should know before taking a CLEP examination what type of credit you can receive and whether you will only be exempted from a required course but receive no credit.

4. How much credit is granted for each examination you are considering, and does the college place a limit on the total amount of CLEP credit you can earn toward your degree?

Not all colleges that grant CLEP credit award the same amount for individual tests. Furthermore, some colleges place a limit on the total amount of credit you can earn through CLEP or other examinations. Other colleges may grant you exemption but no credit toward your degree. Knowing several colleges' policies concerning these issues may help you decide which college you will attend. If you think you are capable of passing a number of CLEP examinations, you may want to attend a college that will allow you to earn credit for all or most of them. For example, the state external degree programs grant credit for most CLEP examinations (and other tests as well).

5. What is the required score for earning CLEP credit for each test you are considering?

Most colleges publish the required scores or percentile ranks for earning CLEP credit in their general catalog or in a brochure. The required score may vary from test to test, so find out the required score for each test you are considering.

6. What is the college's policy regarding prior course work in the subject in which you are considering taking a CLEP test?

Some colleges will not grant credit for a CLEP test if the student has already attempted a college-level course closely aligned with that test. For example, if you successfully completed English 101 or a comparable course on another campus, you will probably not be permitted to receive CLEP credit in that subject, too. Some colleges will not permit you to earn CLEP credit for a course that you failed.

7. Does the college make additional stipulations before credit will be granted?

It is common practice for colleges to award CLEP credit only to their enrolled students. There are other stipulations, however, that vary from college to college. For example, does the college require you to formally apply for or accept CLEP credit by completing and signing a form? Or does the college require you to validate your CLEP score by successfully completing a more advanced course in the subject? Answers to these and other questions will help to smooth the process of earning college credit through CLEP.

The above questions and the discussions that follow them indicate some of the ways in which colleges' CLEP policies can vary. Find out as much as possible about the CLEP policies at the colleges you are interested in so you can choose a college with a policy that is compatible with your educational goals. Once you have selected the college you will attend, you can find out which CLEP examinations your college recognizes and the requirements for earning CLEP credit.

DECIDING WHICH EXAMINATIONS TO TAKE

If You're Taking the Examinations for College Credit or Career Advancement:

Most people who take CLEP examinations do so in order to earn credit for college courses. Others take the examinations in order to qualify for job promotions or for professional certification or licensing. It is vital to most candidates who are taking the tests for any of these reasons that they be well prepared for the tests they are taking so that they can advance as rapidly as possible toward their educational or career goals.

It is usually advisable that those who have limited knowledge in the subjects covered by the tests they are considering enroll in the college courses in which that material is taught. Those who are uncertain about whether or not they know enough about a subject to do well on a particular CLEP test will find the following guidelines helpful.

There is no way to predict if you will pass a particular CLEP examination, but answers to the questions under the seven headings below should give you an indication of whether or not you are likely to succeed.

1. Test Descriptions

Read the description of the test provided. Are you familiar with most of the topics and terminology in the outline?

2. Textbooks

Examine the suggested textbooks and other resource materials following the test descriptions in this guide. Have you recently read one or more of these books, or have you read similar college-level books on this subject? If you have not, read through one or more of the textbooks listed, or through the textbook used for this course at your college. Are you familiar with most of the topics and terminology in the book?

3. Sample Questions

The sample questions provided are intended to be typical of the content and difficulty of the questions on the test. Although they are not an exact miniature of the test, the proportion of the sample questions you can answer correctly should be a rough estimate of the proportion of questions you will be able to answer correctly on the test.

Answer as many of the sample questions for this test as you can. Check your answers against the correct answers. Did you answer more than half the questions correctly?

Because of variations in course content at different institutions, and because questions on CLEP tests vary from easy to difficult - with most being of moderate difficulty - the average student who passes a course in a subject can usually answer correctly about half the questions on the corresponding CLEP examination. Most colleges set their passing scores near this level, but some set them higher. If your college has set its required score above the level required by most colleges, you may need to answer a larger proportion of questions on the test correctly.

4. Previous Study

Have you taken noncredit courses in this subject offered by an adult school or a private school, through correspondence, or in connection with your job? Did you do exceptionally well in this subject in high school, or did you take an honors course in this subject?

5. Experience

Have you learned or used the knowledge or skills included in this test in your job or life experience? For example, if you lived in a Spanish-speaking country and spoke the language for a year or more, you might consider taking the Spanish examination. Or, if you have worked at a job in which you used accounting and finance skills, Principles of Accounting would be a likely test for you to take. Or, if you have read a considerable amount of literature and attended many art exhibits, concerts, and plays, you might expect to do well on the Humanities exam.

6. Other Examinations

Have you done well on other standardized tests in subjects related to the one you want to take? For example, did you score well above average on a portion of a college entrance examination covering similar skills, or did you obtain an exceptionally high score on a high school equivalency test or a licensing examination in this subject? Although such tests do not cover exactly the same material as the CLEP examinations and may be easier, persons who do well on these tests often do well on CLEP examinations, too.

7. Advice

Has a college counselor, professor, or some other professional person familiar with your ability advised you to take a CLEP examination?

If your answer was yes to questions under several of the above headings, you probably have a good chance of passing the CLEP examination you are considering. It is unlikely that you would have acquired sufficient background from experience alone. Learning gained through reading and study is essential, and you will probably find some additional study helpful before taking a CLEP examination.

If You're Taking the Examinations to Prepare for College

Many people entering college, particularly adults returning to college after several years away from formal education, are uncertain about their ability to compete with other college students. They wonder whether they have sufficient background for college study, and those who have been away from formal study for some time wonder whether they have forgotten how to study, how to take tests, and how to write papers. Such people may wish to improve their test-taking and study skills prior to enrolling in courses.

One way to assess your ability to perform at the college level and to improve your test-taking and study skills at the same time is to prepare for and take one or more CLEP examinations. You need not be enrolled in a college to take a CLEP examination, and you may have your scores sent only to yourself and later request that a transcript be sent to a college if you then decide to apply for credit. By reviewing the test descriptions and sample questions, you may find one or several subject areas in which you think you have substantial knowledge. Select one examination, or more if you like, and carefully read at least one of the textbooks listed in the bibliography for the test. By doing this, you will get a better idea of how much you know of what is usually taught in a college-level course in that subject. Study as much material as you can, until you think you have a good grasp of the subject matter. Then take the test at a college in your area. It will be several weeks before you receive your results, and you may wish to begin reviewing for another test in the meantime.

To find out if you are eligible for credit for your CLEP score, you must compare your score with the score required by the college you plan to attend. If you are not yet sure which college you will attend, or whether you will enroll in college at all, you should begin to follow the steps outlined. It is best that you do this before taking a CLEP test, but if you are taking the test only for the experience and to familiarize yourself with college-level material and requirements, you might take the test before you approach a college. Even if the college you decide to attend does not accept the test you took, the experience of taking such a test will enable you to meet with greater confidence the requirements of courses you will take.

You will find information about how to interpret your scores in WHAT YOUR SCORES MEAN, which you will receive with your score report, and which can also be found online at the CLEP website. Many colleges follow the recommendations of the American Council on Education (ACE) for setting their required scores, so you can use this information as a guide in determining how well you did. The ACE recommendations are included in the booklet.

If you do not do well enough on the test to earn college credit, don't be discouraged. Usually, it is the best college students who are exempted from courses or receive credit-by-examination. The fact that you cannot get credit for your score means that you should probably enroll in a college course to learn the material. However, if your score was close to the required score, or if you feel you could do better on a second try or after some additional study, you may retake the test after six months. Do not take it sooner or your score will not be reported and your fee will be forfeited.

If you do earn the score required to earn credit, you will have demonstrated that you already have some college-level knowledge. You will also have a better idea whether you should take additional CLEP examinations. And, what is most important, you can enroll in college with confidence, knowing that you do have the ability to succeed.

PREPARING TO TAKE CLEP EXAMINATIONS

Having made the decision to take one or more CLEP examinations, most people then want to know if it is worthwhile to prepare for them - how much, how long, when, and how should they go about it? The precise answers to these questions vary greatly from individual to individual. However, most candidates find that some type of test preparation is helpful.

Most people who take CLEP examinations do so to show that they have already learned the important material that is taught in a college course. Many of them need only a quick review to assure themselves that they have not forgotten some of what they once studied, and to fill in some of the gaps in their knowledge of the subject. Others feel that they need a thorough review and spend several weeks studying for a test. A few wish to take a CLEP examination as a kind of final examination for independent study of a subject instead of the college course. This last group requires significantly more study than those who only need to review, and they may need some guidance from professors of the subjects they are studying.

The key to how you prepare for CLEP examinations often lies in locating those skills and areas of prior learning in which you are strong and deciding where to focus your energies. Some people may know a great deal about a certain subject area, but may not test well. These individuals would probably be just as concerned about strengthening their test-taking skills as they are about studying for a specific test. Many mental and physical skills are used in preparing for a test. It is important not only to review or study for the examinations, but to make certain that you are alert, relatively free of anxiety, and aware of how to approach standardized tests. Suggestions on developing test-taking skills and preparing psychologically and physically for a test are given. The following section suggests ways of assessing your knowledge of the content of a test and then reviewing and studying the material.

Using This Study Guide

Begin by carefully reading the test description and outline of knowledge and skills required for the examination, if given. As you read through the topics listed there, ask yourself how much you know about each one. Also note the terms, names, and symbols that are mentioned, and ask yourself whether you are familiar with them. This will give you a quick overview of how much you know about the subject. If you are familiar with nearly all the material, you will probably need a minimum of review; however, if less than half of it is familiar, you will probably require substantial study to do well on the test.

If, after reviewing the test description, you find that you need extensive review, delay answering the sample question until you have done some reading in the subject. If you complete them before reviewing the material, you will probably look for the answers as you study, and then they will not be a good assessment of your ability at a later date.

If you think you are familiar with most of the test material, try to answer the sample questions.

Apply the test-taking strategies given. Keeping within the time limit suggested will give you a rough idea of how quickly you should work in order to complete the actual test.

Check your answers against the answer key. If you answered nearly all the questions correctly, you probably do not need to study the subject extensively. If you got about half the questions correct, you ought o review at least one textbook or other suggested materials on the subject. If you answered less than half the questions correctly, you will probably benefit from more extensive reading in the subject and thorough study of one or more textbooks. The textbooks listed are used at many colleges but they are not the only good texts. You will find helpful almost any standard text available to you., such as the textbook used at your college, or earlier editions of texts listed. For some examinations, topic outlines and textbooks may not be available. Take the sample tests in this book and check your answers at the end of each test. Check wrong answers.

Suggestions for Studying

The following suggestions have been gathered from people who have prepared for CLEP examinations or other college-level tests.

1. Define your goals and locate study materials

First, determine your study goals. Set aside a block of time to review the material provided in this book, and then decide which test(s) you will take. Using the suggestions, locate suitable resource materials. If a preparation course is offered by an adult school or college in your area, you might find it helpful to enroll.

2. Find a good place to study

To determine what kind of place you need for studying, ask yourself questions such as: Do I need a quiet place? Does the telephone distract me? Do objects I see in this place remind me of things I should do? Is it too warm? Is it well lit? Am I too comfortable here? Do I have space to spread out my materials? You may find the library more conducive to studying than your home. If you decide to study at home, you might prevent interruptions by other household members by putting a sign on the door of your study room to indicate when you will be available.

3. Schedule time to study

To help you determine where studying best fits into your schedule, try this exercise: Make a list of your daily activities (for example, sleeping, working, and eating) and estimate how many hours per day you spend on each activity. Now, rate all the activities on your list in order of their importance and evaluate your use of time. Often people are astonished at how an average day appears from this perspective. They may discover that they were unaware how large portions of time are spent, or they learn their time can be scheduled in alternative ways. For example, they can remove the least important activities from their day and devote that time to studying or another important activity.

4. Establish a study routine and a set of goals

In order to study effectively, you should establish specific goals and a schedule for accomplishing them. Some people find it helpful to write out a weekly schedule and cross out each study period when it is completed. Others maintain their concentration better by writing down the time when they expect to complete a study task. Most people find short periods of intense study more productive than long stretches of time. For example, they may follow a regular schedule of several 20- or 30-minute study periods with short breaks between them. Some people like to allow themselves rewards as they complete each study goal. It is not essential that you accomplish every goal exactly within your schedule; the point is to be committed to your task.

5. Learn how to take an active role in studying.

If you have not done much studying for some time, you may find it difficult to concentrate at first. Try a method of studying, such as the one outlined below, that will help you concentrate on and remember what you read.

    a. First, read the chapter summary and the introduction. Then you will know what to look for in your reading.

    b. Next, convert the section or paragraph headlines into questions. For example, if you are reading a section entitled, The Causes of the American Revolution, ask yourself: *What were the causes of the American Revolution?* Compose the answer as you read the paragraph. Reading and answering questions aloud will help you understand and remember the material.

c. Take notes on key ideas or concepts as you read. Writing will also help you fix concepts more firmly in your mind. Underlining key ideas or writing notes in your book can be helpful and will be useful for review. Underline only important points. If you underline more than a third of each paragraph, you are probably underlining too much.

d. If there are questions or problems at the end of a chapter, answer or solve them on paper as if you were asked to do them for homework. Mathematics textbooks (and some other books) sometimes include answers to some or all of the exercises. If you have such a book, write your answers before looking at the ones given. When problem-solving is involved, work enough problems to master the required methods and concepts. If you have difficulty with problems, review any sample problems or explanations in the chapter.

e. To retain knowledge, most people have to review the material periodically. If you are preparing for a test over an extended period of time, review key concepts and notes each week or so. Do not wait for weeks to review the material or you will need to relearn much of it.

Psychological and Physical Preparation

Most people feel at least some nervousness before taking a test. Adults who are returning to college may not have taken a test in many years or they may have had little experience with standardized tests. Some younger students, as well, are uncomfortable with testing situations. People who received their education in countries outside the United States may find that many tests given in this country are quite different from the ones they are accustomed to taking.

Not only might candidates find the types of tests and the kinds of questions on them unfamiliar, but other aspects of the testing environment may be strange as well. The physical and mental stress that results from meeting this new experience can hinder a candidate's ability to demonstrate his or her true degree of knowledge in the subject area being tested. For this reason, it is important to go to the test center well prepared, both mentally and physically, for taking the test. You may find the following suggestions helpful.

1. Familiarize yourself, as much as possible, with the test and the test situation before the day of the examination. It will be helpful for you to know ahead of time:

a. How much time will be allowed for the test and whether there are timed subsections.

b. What types of questions and directions appear on the examination.

c. How your test score will be computed.

d. How to properly answer the questions on the computer (See the CLEP Sample on the CLEP website)

e. In which building and room the examination will be administered. If you don't know where the building is, locate it or get directions ahead of time.

f. The time of the test administration. You might wish to confirm this information a day or two before the examination and find out what time the building and room will be open so that you can plan to arrive early.

g. Where to park your car or, if you wish to take public transportation, which bus or train to take and the location of the nearest stop.

h. Whether smoking will be permitted during the test.

i. Whether there will be a break between examinations (if you will be taking more than one on the same day), and whether there is a place nearby where you can get something to eat or drink.

2. Go to the test situation relaxed and alert. In order to prepare for the test:

a. Get a good night's sleep. Last minute cramming, particularly late the night before, is usually counterproductive.

b. Eat normally. It is usually not wise to skip breakfast or lunch on the day of the test or to eat a big meal just before the test.

c. Avoid tranquilizers and stimulants. If you follow the other directions in this book, you won't need artificial aids. It's better to be a little tense than to be drowsy, but stimulants such as coffee and cola can make you nervous and interfere with your concentration.

d. Don't drink a lot of liquids before the test. Having to leave the room during the test will disturb your concentration and take valuable time away from the test.

e. If you are inclined to be nervous or tense, learn some relaxation exercises and use them before and perhaps during the test.

3. Arrive for the test early and prepared. Be sure to:

a. Arrive early enough so that you can find a parking place, locate the test center, and get settled comfortably before testing begins. Allow some extra time in case you are delayed unexpectedly.

b. Take the following with you:

- Your completed Registration/Admission Form
- Two forms of identification – one being a government-issued photo ID with signature, such as a driver's license or passport
- Non-mechanical pencil
- A watch so that you can time your progress (digital watches are prohibited)
- Your glasses if you need them for reading or seeing the chalkboard or wall clock

    c. Leave all books, papers, and notes outside the test center. You will not be permitted to use your own scratch paper; it will be provided. Also prohibited are calculators, cell phones, beepers, pagers, photo/copy devices, radios, headphones, food, beverages, and several other items.

    d. Be prepared for any temperature in the testing room. Wear layers of clothing that can be removed if the room is too hot but will keep you warm if it is too cold.

4. When you enter the test room:

    a. Sit in a seat that provides a maximum of comfort and freedom from distraction.

    b. Read directions carefully, and listen to all instructions given by the test administrator. If you don't understand the directions, ask for help before test timing begins. If you must ask a question after the test has begun, raise your hand and a proctor will assist you. The proctor can answer certain kinds of questions but cannot help you with the test.

    c. Know your rights as a test taker. You can expect to be given the full working time allowed for the test(s) and a reasonably quiet and comfortable place in which to work. If a poor test situation is preventing you from doing your best, ask if the situation can be remedied. If bad test conditions cannot be remedied, ask the person in charge to report the problem in the Irregularity Report that will be sent to ETS with the answer sheets. You may also wish to contact CLEP. Describe the exact circumstances as completely as you can. Be sure to include the test date and name(s) of the test(s) you took. ETS will investigate the problem to make sure it does not happen again, and, if the problem is serious enough, may arrange for you to retake the test without charge.

TAKING THE EXAMINATIONS

A person may know a great deal about the subject being tested, but not do as well as he or she is capable of on the test. Knowing how to approach a test is an important part of the testing process. While a command of test-taking skills cannot substitute for knowledge of the subject matter, it can be a significant factor in successful testing.

Test-taking skills enable a person to use all available information to earn a score that truly reflects his or her ability. There are different strategies for approaching different kinds of test questions. For example, free-response questions require a very different tack than do multiple-choice questions. Other factors, such as how the test will be graded, may also influence your approach to the test and your use of test time. Thus, your preparation for a test should include finding out all you can about the test so that you can use the most effective test-taking strategies.

Before taking a test, you should know approximately how many questions are on the test, how much time you will be allowed, how the test will be scored or graded, what types of questions and directions are on the test, and how you will be required to record your answers.

Taking Multiple-Choice Tests

1. Listen carefully to the instructions given by the test administrator and read carefully all directions before you begin to answer the questions.

2. Note the time that the test administrator starts timing the test. As you proceed, make sure that you are not working too slowly. You should have answered at least half the questions in a section when half the time for that section has passed. If you have not reached that point in the section, speed up your pace on the remaining questions.

3. Before answering a question, read the entire question, including all the answer choices. Don't think that because the first or second answer choice looks good to you, it isn't necessary to read the remaining options. Instructions usually tell you to select the best answer. Sometimes one answer choice is partially correct, but another option is better; therefore, it is usually a good idea to read all the answers before you choose one.

4. Read and consider every question. Questions that look complicated at first glance may not actually be so difficult once you have read them carefully.

5. Do not puzzle too long over any one question. If you don't know the answer after you've considered it briefly, go on to the next question. Make sure you return to the question later.

6. Make sure you record your response properly.

7. In trying to determine the correct answer, you may find it helpful to cross out those options that you know are incorrect, and to make marks next to those you think might be correct. If you decide to skip the question and come back to it later, you will save yourself the time of reconsidering all the options.

8. Watch for the following key words in test questions:

all	generally	never	perhaps
always	however	none	rarely
but	may	not	seldom
except	must	often	sometimes
every	necessary	only	usually

When a question or answer option contains words such as always, every, only, never, and none, there can be no exceptions to the answer you choose. Use of words such as often, rarely, sometimes, and generally indicates that there may be some exceptions to the answer.

9. Do not waste your time looking for clues to right answers based on flaws in question wording or patterns in correct answers. Professionals at the College Board and ETS put

a great deal of effort into developing valid, reliable, fair tests. CLEP test development committees are composed of college faculty who are experts in the subject covered by the test and are appointed by the College Board to write test questions and to scrutinize each question that is included on a CLEP test. Committee members make every effort to ensure that the questions are not ambiguous, that they have only one correct answer, and that they cover college-level topics. These committees do not intentionally include trick questions. If you think a question is flawed, ask the test administrator to report it, or contact CLEP immediately.

Taking Free-Response or Essay Tests

If your college requires the optional free-response or essay portion of a CLEP Composition and Literature exams, you should do some additional preparation for your CLEP test. Taking an essay test is very different from taking a multiple-choice test, so you will need to use some other strategies.

The essay written as part of the English Composition and Essay exam is graded by English professors from a variety of colleges and universities. A process called holistic scoring is used to rate your writing ability.

The optional free-response essays, on the other hand, are graded by the faculty of the college you designate as a score recipient. Guidelines and criteria for grading essays are not specified by the College Board or ETS. You may find it helpful, therefore, to talk with someone at your college to find out what criteria will be used to determine whether you will get credit. If the test requires essay responses, ask how much emphasis will be placed on your writing ability and your ability to organize your thoughts as opposed to your knowledge of subject matter. Find out how much weight will be given to your multiple-choice test score in comparison with your free-response grade in determining whether you will get credit. This will give you an idea where you should expend the greatest effort in preparing for and taking the test.

Here are some strategies you will find useful in taking any essay test:

1. Before you begin to write, read all questions carefully and take a few minutes to jot down some ideas you might include in each answer.

2. If you are given a choice of questions to answer, choose the questions you think you can answer most clearly and knowledgeably.

3. Determine in what order you will answer the questions. Answer those you find the easiest first so that any extra time can be spent on the more difficult questions.

4. When you know which questions you will answer and in what order, determine how much testing time remains and estimate how many minutes you will devote to each question. Unless suggested times are given for the questions or one question appears to require more or less time than the others, allot an equal amount of time to each question.

5. Before answering each question, indicate the number of the question as it is given in the test book. You need not copy the entire question from the question sheet, but it will be helpful to you and to the person grading your test if you indicate briefly the topic you are addressing – particularly if you are not answering the questions in the order in which they appear on the test.

6. Before answering each question, read it again carefully to make sure you are interpreting it correctly. Underline key words, such as those listed below, that often appear in free-response questions. Be sure you know the exact meaning of these words before taking the test.

analyze	demonstrate	enumerate	list
apply	derive	explain	outline
assess	describe	generalize	prove
compare	determine	illustrate	rank
contrast	discuss	interpret	show
define	distinguish	justify	summarize

If a question asks you to outline, define, or summarize, do not write a detailed explanation; if a question asks you to analyze, explain, illustrate, interpret, or show, you must do more than briefly describe the topic.

For a current listing of CLEP Colleges

where you can get credit and be tested, write:

CLEP, P.O. Box 6600, Princeton, NJ 08541-6600

Or e-mail: clep@ets.org, or call: (609) 771-7865

Introduction to Business Management
Principles of Management

Description of the Examination

The Principles of Management examination covers material that is usually taught in an introductory course in the essentials of management and organization. The fact that such courses are offered by different types of institutions and in a number of fields other than business has been taken into account in the preparation of this examination. It requires a knowledge of human resources and operational and functional aspects of management.

The examination contains approximately 100 questions to be answered in 90 minutes. Some of these are pretest questions that will not be scored. Any time candidates spend on tutorials and providing personal information is in addition to the actual testing time.

Knowledge and Skills Required

Questions on the Principles of Management examination require candidates to demonstrate one or more of the following abilities in the approximate proportions indicated.

- Specific factual knowledge, recall, and general understanding of purposes, functions, and techniques of management (about 10 percent of the exam)

- Understanding of and ability to associate the meaning of specific terminology with important management ideas, processes, techniques, concepts, and elements (about 40 percent of the exam)

- Understanding of theory and significant underlying assumptions, concepts, and limitations of management data, including a comprehension of the rationale of procedures, methods, and analyses (about 40 percent of the exam)

- Application of knowledge, general concepts, and principles to specific problems (about 10 percent of the exam)

The subject matter of the Principles of Management examination is drawn from the following topics. The percentages next to the main topics indicate the approximate percentage of exam questions on that topic.

15-25% Organization and Human Resources
- Personnel administration
- Human relations and motivation
- Training and development
- Performance appraisal
- Organizational development
- Legal concerns
- Workforce diversity
- Recruiting and selecting
- Compensation and benefits
- Collective bargaining

From the official announcement for educational purposes

10-20% Operational Aspects of Management
- Operations planning and control
- Work scheduling
- Quality management (e.g., TQM)
- Information processing and management
- Strategic planning and analysis
- Productivity

45-55% Functional Aspects of Management
- Planning
- Organizing
- Leading
- Controlling
- Authority
- Decision making
- Organization charts
- Leadership
- Organizational structure
- Budgeting
- Problem solving
- Group dynamics and team functions
- Conflict resolution
- Communication
- Change
- Organizational theory
- Historical aspects

10-20% International Management and Contemporary Issues
- Value dimensions
- Regional economic integration
- Trading alliances
- Global environment
- Social responsibilities of business
- Ethics
- Systems
- Environment
- Government regulation
- Management theories and theorists
- E-business

HOW TO TAKE A TEST

You have studied long, hard and conscientiously.

With your official admission card in hand, and your heart pounding, you have been admitted to the examination room.

You note that there are several hundred other applicants in the examination room waiting to take the same test.

They all appear to be equally well prepared.

You know that nothing but your best effort will suffice. The "moment of truth" is at hand: you now have to demonstrate objectively, in writing, your knowledge of content and your understanding of subject matter.

You are fighting the most important battle of your life—to pass and/or score high on an examination which will determine your career and provide the economic basis for your livelihood.

What extra, special things should you know and should you do in taking the examination?

I. YOU MUST PASS AN EXAMINATION

A. WHAT EVERY CANDIDATE SHOULD KNOW
Examination applicants often ask us for help in preparing for the written test. What can I study in advance? What kinds of questions will be asked? How will the test be given? How will the papers be graded?

B. HOW ARE EXAMS DEVELOPED?
Examinations are carefully written by trained technicians who are specialists in the field known as "psychological measurement," in consultation with recognized authorities in the field of work that the test will cover. These experts recommend the subject matter areas or skills to be tested; only those knowledges or skills important to your success on the job are included. The most reliable books and source materials available are used as references. Together, the experts and technicians judge the difficulty level of the questions.
Test technicians know how to phrase questions so that the problem is clearly stated. Their ethics do not permit "trick" or "catch" questions. Questions may have been tried out on sample groups, or subjected to statistical analysis, to determine their usefulness.
Written tests are often used in combination with performance tests, ratings of training and experience, and oral interviews. All of these measures combine to form the best-known means of finding the right person for the right job.

II. HOW TO PASS THE WRITTEN TEST

A. BASIC STEPS

1) Study the announcement

How, then, can you know what subjects to study? Our best answer is: "Learn as much as possible about the class of positions for which you've applied." The exam will test the knowledge, skills and abilities needed to do the work.

Your most valuable source of information about the position you want is the official exam announcement. This announcement lists the training and experience qualifications. Check these standards and apply only if you come reasonably close to meeting them. Many jurisdictions preview the written test in the exam announcement by including a section called "Knowledge and Abilities Required," "Scope of the Examination," or some similar heading. Here you will find out specifically what fields will be tested.

2) Choose appropriate study materials

If the position for which you are applying is technical or advanced, you will read more advanced, specialized material. If you are already familiar with the basic principles of your field, elementary textbooks would waste your time. Concentrate on advanced textbooks and technical periodicals. Think through the concepts and review difficult problems in your field.

These are all general sources. You can get more ideas on your own initiative, following these leads. For example, training manuals and publications of the government agency which employs workers in your field can be useful, particularly for technical and professional positions. A letter or visit to the government department involved may result in more specific study suggestions, and certainly will provide you with a more definite idea of the exact nature of the position you are seeking.

3) Study this book!

III. KINDS OF TESTS

Tests are used for purposes other than measuring knowledge and ability to perform specified duties. For some positions, it is equally important to test ability to make adjustments to new situations or to profit from training. In others, basic mental abilities not dependent on information are essential. Questions which test these things may not appear as pertinent to the duties of the position as those which test for knowledge and information. Yet they are often highly important parts of a fair examination. For very general questions, it is almost impossible to help you direct your study efforts. What we can do is to point out some of the more common of these general abilities needed in public service positions and describe some typical questions.

1) General information

Broad, general information has been found useful for predicting job success in some kinds of work. This is tested in a variety of ways, from vocabulary lists to questions about current events. Basic background in some field of work, such as sociology or economics, may be sampled in a group of questions. Often these are principles which have become familiar to most persons through exposure rather than through formal training. It is difficult to advise you how to study for these questions; being alert to the world around you is our best suggestion.

2) Verbal ability

An example of an ability needed in many positions is verbal or language ability. Verbal ability is, in brief, the ability to use and understand words. Vocabulary and grammar tests are typical measures of this ability. Reading comprehension or paragraph interpretation questions are common in many kinds of civil service tests. You are given a paragraph of written material and asked to find its central meaning.

IV. KINDS OF QUESTIONS

1. Multiple-choice Questions

Most popular of the short-answer questions is the "multiple choice" or "best answer" question. It can be used, for example, to test for factual knowledge, ability to solve problems or judgment in meeting situations found at work.

A multiple-choice question is normally one of three types:
- It can begin with an incomplete statement followed by several possible endings. You are to find the one ending which best completes the statement, although some of the others may not be entirely wrong.
- It can also be a complete statement in the form of a question which is answered by choosing one of the statements listed.
- It can be in the form of a problem – again you select the best answer.

Here is an example of a multiple-choice question with a discussion which should give you some clues as to the method for choosing the right answer:

When an employee has a complaint about his assignment, the action which will best help him overcome his difficulty is to
    A. discuss his difficulty with his coworkers
    B. take the problem to the head of the organization
    C. take the problem to the person who gave him the assignment
    D. say nothing to anyone about his complaint

In answering this question, you should study each of the choices to find which is best. Consider choice "A" – Certainly an employee may discuss his complaint with fellow employees, but no change or improvement can result, and the complaint remains unresolved. Choice "B" is a poor choice since the head of the organization probably does not know what assignment you have been given, and taking your problem to him is known as "going over the head" of the supervisor. The supervisor, or person who made the assignment, is the person who can clarify it or correct any injustice. Choice "C" is, therefore, correct. To say nothing, as in choice "D," is unwise. Supervisors have and interest in knowing the problems employees are facing, and the employee is seeking a solution to his problem.

2. True/False

3. Matching Questions

Matching an answer from a column of choices within another column.

V. RECORDING YOUR ANSWERS

Computer terminals are used more and more today for many different kinds of exams.

For an examination with very few applicants, you may be told to record your answers in the test booklet itself. Separate answer sheets are much more common. If this separate answer sheet is to be scored by machine – and this is often the case – it is highly important that you mark your answers correctly in order to get credit.

VI. BEFORE THE TEST

YOUR PHYSICAL CONDITION IS IMPORTANT

If you are not well, you can't do your best work on tests. If you are half asleep, you can't do your best either. Here are some tips:

1) Get about the same amount of sleep you usually get. Don't stay up all night before the test, either partying or worrying—DON'T DO IT!
2) If you wear glasses, be sure to wear them when you go to take the test. This goes for hearing aids, too.
3) If you have any physical problems that may keep you from doing your best, be sure to tell the person giving the test. If you are sick or in poor health, you relay cannot do your best on any test. You can always come back and take the test some other time.

Common sense will help you find procedures to follow to get ready for an examination. Too many of us, however, overlook these sensible measures. Indeed, nervousness and fatigue have been found to be the most serious reasons why applicants fail to do their best on civil service tests. Here is a list of reminders:

- Begin your preparation early – Don't wait until the last minute to go scurrying around for books and materials or to find out what the position is all about.
- Prepare continuously – An hour a night for a week is better than an all-night cram session. This has been definitely established. What is more, a night a week for a month will return better dividends than crowding your study into a shorter period of time.
- Locate the place of the exam – You have been sent a notice telling you when and where to report for the examination. If the location is in a different town or otherwise unfamiliar to you, it would be well to inquire the best route and learn something about the building.
- Relax the night before the test – Allow your mind to rest. Do not study at all that night. Plan some mild recreation or diversion; then go to bed early and get a good night's sleep.
- Get up early enough to make a leisurely trip to the place for the test – This way unforeseen events, traffic snarls, unfamiliar buildings, etc. will not upset you.
- Dress comfortably – A written test is not a fashion show. You will be known by number and not by name, so wear something comfortable.
- Leave excess paraphernalia at home – Shopping bags and odd bundles will get in your way. You need bring only the items mentioned in the official notice you received; usually everything you need is provided. Do not bring reference books to the exam. They will only confuse those last minutes and be taken away from you when in the test room.

- Arrive somewhat ahead of time – If because of transportation schedules you must get there very early, bring a newspaper or magazine to take your mind off yourself while waiting.
- Locate the examination room – When you have found the proper room, you will be directed to the seat or part of the room where you will sit. Sometimes you are given a sheet of instructions to read while you are waiting. Do not fill out any forms until you are told to do so; just read them and be prepared.
- Relax and prepare to listen to the instructions
- If you have any physical problem that may keep you from doing your best, be sure to tell the test administrator. If you are sick or in poor health, you really cannot do your best on the exam. You can come back and take the test some other time.

VII. AT THE TEST

The day of the test is here and you have the test booklet in your hand. The temptation to get going is very strong. Caution! There is more to success than knowing the right answers. You must know how to identify your papers and understand variations in the type of short-answer question used in this particular examination. Follow these suggestions for maximum results from your efforts:

1) Cooperate with the monitor

The test administrator has a duty to create a situation in which you can be as much at ease as possible. He will give instructions, tell you when to begin, check to see that you are marking your answer sheet correctly, and so on. He is not there to guard you, although he will see that your competitors do not take unfair advantage. He wants to help you do your best.

2) Listen to all instructions

Don't jump the gun! Wait until you understand all directions. In most civil service tests you get more time than you need to answer the questions. So don't be in a hurry. Read each word of instructions until you clearly understand the meaning. Study the examples, listen to all announcements and follow directions. Ask questions if you do not understand what to do.

3) Identify your papers

Civil service exams are usually identified by number only. You will be assigned a number; you must not put your name on your test papers. Be sure to copy your number correctly. Since more than one exam may be given, copy your exact examination title.

4) Plan your time

Unless you are told that a test is a "speed" or "rate of work" test, speed itself is usually not important. Time enough to answer all the questions will be provided, but this does not mean that you have all day. An overall time limit has been set. Divide the total time (in minutes) by the number of questions to determine the approximate time you have for each question.

5) Do not linger over difficult questions

If you come across a difficult question, mark it with a paper clip (useful to have along) and come back to it when you have been through the booklet. One caution if you do this – be sure to skip a number on your answer sheet as well. Check often to be sure that you have not lost your place and that you are marking in the row numbered the same as the question you are answering.

6) Read the questions

Be sure you know what the question asks! Many capable people are unsuccessful because they failed to read the questions correctly.

7) Answer all questions

Unless you have been instructed that a penalty will be deducted for incorrect answers, it is better to guess than to omit a question.

8) Speed tests

It is often better NOT to guess on speed tests. It has been found that on timed tests people are tempted to spend the last few seconds before time is called in marking answers at random – without even reading them – in the hope of picking up a few extra points. To discourage this practice, the instructions may warn you that your score will be "corrected" for guessing. That is, a penalty will be applied. The incorrect answers will be deducted from the correct ones, or some other penalty formula will be used.

9) Review your answers

If you finish before time is called, go back to the questions you guessed or omitted to give them further thought. Review other answers if you have time.

10) Return your test materials

If you are ready to leave before others have finished or time is called, take ALL your materials to the monitor and leave quietly. Never take any test material with you. The monitor can discover whose papers are not complete, and taking a test booklet may be grounds for disqualification.

VIII. EXAMINATION TECHNIQUES

1) Read the general instructions carefully. These are usually printed on the first page of the exam booklet. As a rule, these instructions refer to the timing of the examination; the fact that you should not start work until the signal and must stop work at a signal, etc. If there are any special instructions, such as a choice of questions to be answered, make sure that you note this instruction carefully.

2) When you are ready to start work on the examination, that is as soon as the signal has been given, read the instructions to each question booklet, underline any key words or phrases, such as least, best, outline, describe and the like. In this way you will tend to answer as requested rather than discover on reviewing your paper that you listed without describing, that you selected the worst choice rather than the best choice, etc.

3) If the examination is of the objective or multiple-choice type – that is, each question will also give a series of possible answers: A, B, C or D, and you are called upon to select the best answer and write the letter next to that answer on your answer paper – it is advisable to start answering each question in turn. There may be anywhere from 50 to 100 such questions in the three or four hours allotted and you can see how much time would be taken if you read through all the questions before beginning to answer any. Furthermore, if you

come across a question or group of questions which you know would be difficult to answer, it would undoubtedly affect your handling of all the other questions.

4) If the examination is of the essay type and contains but a few questions, it is a moot point as to whether you should read all the questions before starting to answer any one. Of course, if you are given a choice – say five out of seven and the like – then it is essential to read all the questions so you can eliminate the two that are most difficult. If, however, you are asked to answer all the questions, there may be danger in trying to answer the easiest one first because you may find that you will spend too much time on it. The best technique is to answer the first question, then proceed to the second, etc.

5) Time your answers. Before the exam begins, write down the time it started, then add the time allowed for the examination and write down the time it must be completed, then divide the time available somewhat as follows:
    - If 3-1/2 hours are allowed, that would be 210 minutes. If you have 80 objective-type questions, that would be an average of 2-1/2 minutes per question. Allow yourself no more than 2 minutes per question, or a total of 160 minutes, which will permit about 50 minutes to review.
    - If for the time allotment of 210 minutes there are 7 essay questions to answer, that would average about 30 minutes a question. Give yourself only 25 minutes per question so that you have about 35 minutes to review.

6) The most important instruction is to read each question and make sure you know what is wanted. The second most important instruction is to time yourself properly so that you answer every question. The third most important instruction is to answer every question. Guess if you have to but include something for each question. Remember that you will receive no credit for a blank and will probably receive some credit if you write something in answer to an essay question. If you guess a letter – say "B" for a multiple-choice question – you may have guessed right. If you leave a blank as an answer to a multiple-choice question, the examiners may respect your feelings but it will not add a point to your score. Some exams may penalize you for wrong answers, so in such cases only, you may not want to guess unless you have some basis for your answer.

7) Suggestions
   a. Objective-type questions
      1. Examine the question booklet for proper sequence of pages and questions
      2. Read all instructions carefully
      3. Skip any question which seems too difficult; return to it after all other questions have been answered
      4. Apportion your time properly; do not spend too much time on any single question or group of questions
      5. Note and underline key words – all, most, fewest, least, best, worst, same, opposite, etc.
      6. Pay particular attention to negatives
      7. Note unusual option, e.g., unduly long, short, complex, different or similar in content to the body of the question
      8. Observe the use of "hedging" words – probably, may, most likely, etc.

9. Make sure that your answer is put next to the same number as the question
10. Do not second-guess unless you have good reason to believe the second answer is definitely more correct
11. Cross out original answer if you decide another answer is more accurate; do not erase until you are ready to hand your paper in
12. Answer all questions; guess unless instructed otherwise
13. Leave time for review

b. Essay questions
   1. Read each question carefully
   2. Determine exactly what is wanted. Underline key words or phrases.
   3. Decide on outline or paragraph answer
   4. Include many different points and elements unless asked to develop any one or two points or elements
   5. Show impartiality by giving pros and cons unless directed to select one side only
   6. Make and write down any assumptions you find necessary to answer the questions
   7. Watch your English, grammar, punctuation and choice of words
   8. Time your answers; don't crowd material

8) Answering the essay question

Most essay questions can be answered by framing the specific response around several key words or ideas. Here are a few such key words or ideas:

M's: manpower, materials, methods, money, management
P's: purpose, program, policy, plan, procedure, practice, problems, pitfalls, personnel, public relations

a. Six basic steps in handling problems:
   1. Preliminary plan and background development
   2. Collect information, data and facts
   3. Analyze and interpret information, data and facts
   4. Analyze and develop solutions as well as make recommendations
   5. Prepare report and sell recommendations
   6. Install recommendations and follow up effectiveness

b. Pitfalls to avoid
1. Taking things for granted – A statement of the situation does not necessarily imply that each of the elements is necessarily true; for example, a complaint may be invalid and biased so that all that can be taken for granted is that a complaint has been registered
2. Considering only one side of a situation – Wherever possible, indicate several alternatives and then point out the reasons you selected the best one
3. Failing to indicate follow up – Whenever your answer indicates action on your part, make certain that you will take proper follow-up action to see how successful your recommendations, procedures or actions turn out to be
4. Taking too long in answering any single question – Remember to time your answers properly

EXAMINATION SECTION

EXAMINATION SECTION
TEST 1

DIRECTIONS: Each question or incomplete statement is followed by several suggested answers or completions. Select the one that BEST answers the question or completes the statement. *PRINT THE LETTER OF THE CORRECT ANSWER IN THE SPACE AT THE RIGHT.*

1. In production and operations control, choosing the site of the production facility is a function of the _____ process.   1._____

    A. production design
    B. selection
    C. production planning
    D. production evaluation

2. Each of the following is an advantage associated with high job specialization EXCEPT for   2._____

    A. facilitating scientific method study
    B. saving time in switching from one task to another
    C. being well-suited to small, entrepreneurial companies
    D. increasing worker dexterity

3. A statement of the duties, working conditions, and other significant requirements associated with a particular job is termed a   3._____

    A. replacement chart
    B. job specification
    C. job description
    D. job analysis

4. A _____ organizational plan is illustrated by a company's method for figuring overtime pay.   4._____

    A. short-term
    B. long-term
    C. single-use
    D. standing

5. Which of the following files lists the names and quantities of all items that are required to produce one unit of product?   5._____

    A. Inventory
    B. Output
    C. MRP
    D. Bill of materials

6. Which of the following is NOT a branch of the quantitative management approach?   6._____

    A. Behavioral science
    B. Management information systems
    C. Operations management
    D. Management science

7. During a staff development meeting, several employees are asked to view some videotapes that illustrate a process related to job performance, and are then asked to tape and observe their own performance of this activity.
This is an example of   7._____

    A. understudy
    B. socialization
    C. behavior modeling
    D. apprenticeship

8. _____ is a statistical technique that involves evaluating random samples from a group of produced materials to determine whether the group meets agreeable quality levels.

   A. Statistical process control
   B. Acceptance sampling
   C. Raw materials sampling
   D. AQL

9. A formal business group, consisting of a manager and all the subordinates who report to that manager, is known as a(n)

   A. strategic business unit   B. reference group
   C. command group   D. module

10. Which of the following ideas was contributed by the classical viewpoint of management?

    A. The visualization of organizations as systems of interrelated parts
    B. The managerial importance of leadership
    C. There is no one best way to manage
    D. The importance of pay as a motivator

11. Each of the following is a component of quality control EXCEPT

    A. marketability   B. function
    C. aesthetics   D. safety

12. The human resource needs of a company are determined *primarily* by

    A. a human resource audit
    B. the company's goals and strategies
    C. the legal environment
    D. a replacement chart

13. If an employee is terminated as a result of _____, this is an example of *due cause*.

    A. layoff   B. incompetence
    C. retirement   D. plant closing

14. According to the systems approach to management, there are four major components to an organizational system. Which of the following is NOT one of these components?

    A. Inputs   B. Transformation processes
    C. Feedback   D. Raw materials

15. Tactical problems are *primarily* the responsibility of

    A. workers   B. low-level managers
    C. middle-level managers   D. executives

16. Robert Owens' (1771–1858) contribution to management theory involved

    A. human resources   B. cognitive theory
    C. work specialization   D. behaviorist theory

17. The _____ dimension of quality involves the degree to which a product's design or operating characteristics meet established standards.   17._____

    A. reliability
    B. conformance
    C. serviceability
    D. durability

18. Which type of technology is illustrated by a commercial bank?   18._____

    A. Long–linked
    B. Intensive
    C. Long–term
    D. Mediating

19. According to situational leadership theory, the technique of *telling* is used when followers are   19._____

    A. able to take responsibility but are unwilling or too insecure to do so
    B. able and willing to take responsibility
    C. unable to take responsibility but are willing to do so
    D. unable and unwilling or too insecure to take responsibility for a given task

20. The principles of management by objectives (MBO) include each of the following EXCEPT   20._____

    A. executive–proposed goals
    B. managerial–subordinate discussion
    C. mutual goal–setting
    D. performance feedback

21. Each of the following is considered to be a valuable characteristic of layout design EXCEPT   21._____

    A. reduction of material transport cost, but not time
    B. bottleneck–free floor design
    C. employee safety provisions
    D. minimizing travel distance required for worker to reach materials

22. What stage of group development deals with accomplishing assigned tasks?   22._____

    A. Internal problem–solving
    B. Growth and productivity
    C. Orientation
    D. Evaluation and control

23. Typically, which of the following steps in the budgetary process would occur FIRST?   23._____

    A. Unit manager formulation of unit's operating plans
    B. Top management outlines resource restraints
    C. Top management combines information
    D. Unit managers determine resource needs

24. In a matching analysis, what has occurred when an external opportunity matches the internal strength of a company?

    A. Problem
    B. Vulnerability
    C. Leverage
    D. Constraint

25. What type of reinforcement schedule is illustrated by a weekly paycheck?

    A. Variable interval
    B. Variable ratio
    C. Fixed interval
    D. Fixed ratio

KEY (CORRECT ANSWERS)

1.	B	11.	A
2.	C	12.	B
3.	C	13.	B
4.	D	14.	D
5.	D	15.	C
6.	A	16.	A
7.	C	17.	B
8.	B	18.	D
9.	C	19.	D
10.	D	20.	A

21. A
22. B
23. B
24. C
25. C

TEST 2

DIRECTIONS: Each question or incomplete statement is followed by several suggested answers or completions. Select the one that BEST answers the question or completes the statement. *PRINT THE LETTER OF THE CORRECT ANSWER IN THE SPACE AT THE RIGHT.*

1. A management approach that is oblivious to ethical considerations is described as   1._____

   A. unethical   B. amoral   C. libertine   D. immoral

2. Informal leaders could serve a valuable role in a company when   2._____

   A. they defer to organizational power
   B. their influence is compatible with the company's goals
   C. they make other people feel satisfied with their own performance
   D. their activity receives praise from higher management

3. Moving from marketing to production is an example of a(n) _____ of career path.   3._____

   A. vertical   B. circumferential
   C. radial   D. cone

4. Each of the following is a DISADVANTAGE associated with the use of a rational model for decision-making in a company EXCEPT   4._____

   A. preferences cannot be ranked in a permanent way
   B. payoffs are difficult to estimate
   C. not all necessary information is available
   D. environmental conditions cannot be accurately forecast

5. The MAIN advantage to product departmentalization is   5._____

   A. duplication of efforts
   B. adaptability
   C. achieving economies of scale
   D. innovation

6. The decision to hire a new employee is a(n) _____ decision.   6._____

   A. programmed   B. nonprogrammed
   C. detail   D. under certainty

7. Which of the following are concerned with departmental or interdepartmental activities?   7._____

   A. Policies   B. Procedures
   C. Rules   D. Goals and strategies

8. Each of the following is a legal concern associated with job testing EXCEPT   8._____

   A. length of the test
   B. reliability of the test
   C. relation of test to the job
   D. whether test measures what it professes to measure

9. The settling of disputes over contract language during collective bargaining is known as _____ arbitration.   9._____

   A. interest   B. verbal   C. rights   D. contract

10. In an oligopolistic economic environment, there are _____ sellers and _____ buyers.

    A. many; few
    B. many; many
    C. few; many
    D. few; few

11. What term would be used to describe a company whose decision-making power is dispersed among lower-level managers?

    A. Thin
    B. Decentralized
    C. Flat
    D. Fat

12. The effort to solve problems by beginning with a problem and attempting to move logically to a solution is known as

    A. the rational model
    B. convergent thinking
    C. the incremental model
    D. divergent thinking

13. If a manager determines that controls are needed but the control process will be too costly, each of the following is an alternative to controls EXCEPT

    A. changing the dependence relationship
    B. implementing horizontal integration
    C. changing organizational goals and objectives to eliminate dependence
    D. changing the nature of the dependence

14. Each of the following is an advantage associated with the use of internal recruitment in the management of human resources EXCEPT

    A. availability of reliable candidate information
    B. rewarding of good performance
    C. increased internal morale due to upward mobility opportunities
    D. increased likelihood of new ideas being introduced

15. A company uses an organizational design in which a product structure overlays a functional structure. What type of design structure is being used?

    A. Functional
    B. Matrix
    C. Contingency
    D. Classical

16. The allocation of a company's financial resources is known as the _____ process.

    A. capital development
    B. financial evaluation
    C. budgeting
    D. equity sourcing

17. Developing plans, setting goals, and making decisions are part of

    A. coordination
    B. influencing
    C. formulation
    D. implementation

18. Generally, the consumerism movement is concerned with each of the following EXCEPT

    A. price fixing
    B. retail complaint-handling
    C. equal opportunity employment
    D. deceptive labeling

19. A company's management sets a goal of achieving a 12% return on investment capital from the sale of a company's product line. What type of goal has the company set?

    A. Operative
    B. Official
    C. Operational
    D. Short-term

20. When a company's turnover rate is too low,

    A. replacement costs are too high
    B. there has been blocking of lower-level personnel
    C. insufficient weeding out has taken place
    D. a shortage of capable managers exists

21. A ratio that compares the owner's financial contributions to a company with creditors' contributions is called the _____ ratio.

    A. leverage
    B. profitability
    C. liquidity
    D. operating

22. The production evaluation process is primarily concerned with _____ control.

    A. input
    B. output
    C. marginal
    D. process

23. _____ is considered a structural barrier to managerial automation.

    A. Incompatible systems
    B. Uncertainty avoidance
    C. Resistance
    D. A reward system that emphasizes quick and dramatic results

24. After an affirmative action plan has been written by a reporting company, a copy is required to be forwarded to the

    A. Department of Labor
    B. Equal Employment Opportunity Commission (EEOC)
    C. National Labor Relations Board
    D. Department of Human Service

25. Historically, the management theory that first focused on principles that could be used by managers to coordinate the internal activities of organizations was the theory of _____ management.

    A. behaviorist
    B. quantitative
    C. administrative
    D. bureaucratic

KEY (CORRECT ANSWERS)

1.	B		11.	B
2.	B		12.	B
3.	B		13.	B
4.	C		14.	D
5.	B		15.	B
6.	A		16.	C
7.	B		17.	C
8.	A		18.	C
9.	A		19.	A
10.	C		20.	C

21. A
22. B
23. D
24. A
25. C

TEST 3

DIRECTIONS: Each question or incomplete statement is followed by several suggested answers or completions. Select the one that BEST answers the question or completes the statement. *PRINT THE LETTER OF THE CORRECT ANSWER IN THE SPACE AT THE RIGHT.*

1. Which of the following is a financial resource for a company? 1.____
   A. Raw material reserves
   B. Reputation for quality
   C. Bond issues
   D. Warehouses

2. Discretionary expense centers are LEAST likely to be used with _____ departments. 2.____
   A. finance
   B. human resources
   C. research and development
   D. public relations

3. _____ managerial power is said to come from the individual, rather than from the company. 3.____
   A. Coercive
   B. Reward
   C. Expert
   D. Legitimate

4. The data inputs to computer–based executive support–systems are probably 4.____
   A. transactions
   B. aggregate data
   C. high–volume data
   D. analytic models

5. What type of audit involves the evaluation and assessment of an entire company's operations? 5.____
   A. Management
   B. Social
   C. External
   D. Internal

6. Performance feedback that is NOT evaluative is described as 6.____
   A. informal
   B. reinforcing
   C. dispersed
   D. informational

7. Which type of leader power stems from a position's placement in the managerial hierarchy and the authority vested in the position? 7.____
   A. Legitimate
   B. Referent
   C. Expert
   D. Reward

8. In matrix organizations, the BEST strategy for conflict resolution is typically 8.____
   A. conciliation
   B. consensus
   C. confrontation
   D. aversion

9. Which of the following is a destructive force that is MOST likely to affect the implementation phase of the development of a quality circle? 9.____
   A. Disagreement on problems
   B. Raised aspirations
   C. Prohibitive costs
   D. Burnout

10. An accountant who audits a company's books would use the _____ style of decision-making.   10.___

    A. intuitive
    B. systematic
    C. compensatory
    D. preceptive

11. Which functional area of a company involves equity ratio?   11.___

    A. Finance
    B. Marketing
    C. Operations
    D. Development

12. A company's plan for the acquisition or divestiture of major fixed assets is the   12.___

    A. profit budget
    B. balance sheet
    C. expense budget
    D. capital expenditures budget

13. The main DISADVANTAGE associated with job simplification is   13.___

    A. higher training costs
    B. lack of quality control mechanism
    C. lowered employee motivation
    D. loss of production efficiency

14. A company uses a compensation system in which employees throughout the organization are encouraged to become involved in solving problems, and are given bonuses tied to organizational performance improvements.   14.___
    This is an example of

    A. skill-based pay
    B. gainsharing
    C. benchmarking
    D. expanded commission

15. A task force formed by a company is responsible to   15.___

    A. the local community
    B. top-level management
    C. union leaders
    D. stockholders

16. What is the term for the identification of a trend and smoothing its pattern?   16.___

    A. Segmentation
    B. Moving average
    C. Time-series analysis
    D. Replacement analysis

17. _____ is a term for grouping jobs horizontally.   17.___

    A. Aggregation
    B. Departmentalization
    C. Formalization
    D. Dispersion

18. Which type of power, if exercised by a manager, is MOST likely to result in resistance by subordinates?   18.___

    A. Reward   B. Expert   C. Coercive   D. Referent

19. In manufacturing, MRP systems use three major inputs. Which of the following is NOT one of these three?

    A. Bill of materials information
    B. Investment information
    C. Inventory status information
    D. Master production schedule

20. What type of quality control is concerned *primarily* with the quality of raw input materials?

    A. Output
    B. Feed–forward
    C. Feedback
    D. Work in process

21. When groups are slow to reach a decision, they are demonstrating

    A. assembly effect
    B. entropy
    C. process loss
    D. synergy

22. ____ costs are those associated with acquiring raw materials.

    A. Storage
    B. Contingency
    C. Order
    D. Carrying

23. An effective managerial control system is each of the following EXCEPT

    A. focused
    B. flexible
    C. future–oriented
    D. timely

24. During what stage of orientation does an employee acquire technical skills that are likely to improve her current job performance?

    A. Induction
    B. Implementation
    C. Socialization
    D. Training

25. In a bureaucracy, the practice of adding unnecessary subordinates is likely to create

    A. red tape
    B. position protection
    C. dominance of authority
    D. inflexibility

KEY (CORRECT ANSWERS)

1. C
2. A
3. C
4. B
5. A
6. D
7. A
8. C
9. C
10. B

11. A
12. D
13. C
14. B
15. B
16. C
17. B
18. C
19. B
20. B

21. C
22. C
23. A
24. D
25. C

EXAMINATION SECTION
TEST 1

DIRECTIONS: Each question or incomplete statement is followed by several suggested answers or completions. Select the one that BEST answers the question or completes the statement. *PRINT THE LETTER OF THE CORRECT ANSWER IN THE SPACE AT THE RIGHT.*

Questions 1-2.

DIRECTIONS: Questions 1 and 2 refer to the information below.
An automobile manufacturer estimates a total annual demand of 60,000 axles for use in the manufacturing process, ordering costs of $30 per order, and holding costs of $20 per unit per year. The lead time for obtaining axles from a nearby producer is 8 days. The equation for determining EOQ is as follows:

$$EOQ = \frac{\sqrt{2(\text{demand})(\text{ordering costs})}}{(\text{holding costs})}$$

1. Using the economic order quantity of (EOQ) equation for inventory control, what is the company's approximate EOQ?

   A. 225   B. 425   C. 90,000   D. 180,000

2. The reorder point, or inventory level at which a new order should be placed, is determined by the following equation:
   ROP = (lead time)(demand ÷ 365).
   According to the information above, an inventory manager should place a new order when the stock of axles reaches approximately

   A. 425   B. 658   C. 1315   D. 2630

3. When speed and accuracy are important and a task is complex, _____ communication is probably the best method.

   A. circle   B. chain
   C. wheel   D. all-channel

4. When a job selection rate for a protected group is less than 80 percent of the rate for the majority group, _____ has occurred.

   A. adverse impact   B. affirmative action
   C. adverse selection   D. discrimination

5. Which of the following is NOT an advantage associated with functional job grouping?

   A. Establishes cost centers for easier financial control
   B. Allows for specialization
   C. Facilitates coordination by top managers
   D. Demonstrates clearly-marked career paths

6. The Taft-Hartley Act is a piece of federal legislation that regulates

   A. equal employment opportunities
   B. employee compensation
   C. labor-management relations
   D. insider stock trading

7. A company's manufacturing and shipping departments usually exhibit _____ interdependence.

   A. sequential
   B. integrated
   C. tangential
   D. applied

8. Which type of plant layout pattern is illustrated by an airplane production plant?

   A. Product
   B. Process
   C. Fixed-position
   D. Input

9. The purpose of an ombudsperson is to

   A. initiate single-action plans
   B. coordinate market research data
   C. alleviate channel conflict
   D. handle employee grievances and ethical problems

10. A raw materials inventory is a stock of

    A. items that are currently being transformed into a final product or service
    B. parts, ingredients, and other basic inputs to a production or service process
    C. materials that are used to facilitate production or to satisfy customer demand
    D. items that have been produced and are awaiting sale or transit

11. In Herzberg's theory, fringe benefits are an example of a(n) _____ factor.

    A. satisfying
    B. motivating
    C. physiological
    D. hygiene

12. Market research data suggest that a company's product is no longer competitive in quality or price. However, the company still hopes to maintain its current sales for the product. What type of strategy would be BEST for this product?

    A. Shrink
    B. Defense
    C. Turnaround
    D. Growth

13. Each of the following is a physical resource for a company EXCEPT

    A. managerial personnel
    B. raw material reserves
    C. manufacturing plant efficiency
    D. location of physical plants

14. The diagram showing the authority and responsibility relationships within a company is the _____ chart.

    A. Gantt
    B. replacement
    C. organization
    D. succession

15. Which of the following is not typically classified as a carrying cost?

    A. Breakage   B. Spoilage   C. Postage   D. Insurance

16. *External equity* is the term for the extent to which   16._____
    A. pay rates allocated to specific individuals within the organization reflect variations in individual merit
    B. pay rates for particular jobs correspond to rates paid for similar jobs on the entire job market
    C. pay rates for various jobs inside the organization reflect the relative worth of those jobs
    D. compensable factors will be used to rate the worth of particular jobs

17. The PRIMARY goal of an amoral manager is   17._____
    A. optimum market share   B. public service
    C. profitability   D. organizational success

18. What is the term for a predetermined standard against which random samples of produced materials are compared in acceptance sampling?   18._____
    A. Statistical product control
    B. Acceptable quality level
    C. Quality circle
    D. Finished goods inventory

19. As the need for coordination increases within a company, what type of job grouping becomes most beneficial?   19._____
    A. Functional   B. Geographic
    C. Process   D. Product

20. Which of the following is not one of a company's human resources?   20._____
    A. Sales representatives
    B. Engineers
    C. Customers
    D. Computer systems analysts

21. Which of the following types of interdependency is emphasized by long-linked technology?   21._____
    A. Reciprocal   B. Pooled
    C. Sequential   D. Applied

22. At the managerial level, the mentoring relationship is an example of the _____ technique for learning technical skills.   22._____
    A. OJT   B. understudy
    C. socialization   D. induction

23. Which of the following is NOT an element of MacGregor's Theory Y concerning managerial assumptions?   23._____
    A. When conditions are favorable, the average person will seek responsibility.
    B. Commitment to goals is the function of available rewards.
    C. The average person wants to be directed, and seeks security above all.
    D. The intellectual potential of most workers is only partially utilized in most companies.

24. Which of the following is a DISADVANTAGE associated with group decision-making? 24.___

    A. High cost
    B. Less careful evaluation of alternatives
    C. Deterioration of group member skills
    D. Less thorough problem identification

25. What is another term for an operating plan? 25.___

    A. SBU plan B. Daily plan
    C. Functional plan D. Tactical plan

KEY (CORRECT ANSWERS)

1.	B	11.	D
2.	C	12.	A
3.	B	13.	A
4.	A	14.	C
5.	C	15.	C
6.	C	16.	B
7.	A	17.	C
8.	C	18.	B
9.	D	19.	D
10.	B	20.	C

21. C
22. B
23. C
24. A
25. D

TEST 2

DIRECTIONS: Each question or incomplete statement is followed by several suggested answers or completions. Select the one that BEST answers the question or completes the statement. *PRINT THE LETTER OF THE CORRECT ANSWER IN THE SPACE AT THE RIGHT.*

1. According to the contingency model of leadership, which of the following factors is MOST significant in affecting a leader's favorability?

    A. Leader-member relations
    B. Personality traits
    C. Task structure
    D. Position power

2. Each of the following is an element of organization structure EXCEPT the

    A. various mechanisms needed to foster vertical coordination
    B. clustering of individual positions into units, and of units into departments, to form a hierarchy
    C. assignment of tasks and responsibilities that define individual and unit jobs
    D. working capital available for expansion of unit and departmental functions

3. _____ analysis centers on what a company is able to do.

    A. Regression
    B. Internal resource
    C. P&L
    D. Trend

4. Which of the following leadership theories emphasizes the individual characteristics of leaders?

    A. Situational
    B. Actualization
    C. Behavioral
    D. Trait

5. Which of the following management theories is NOT a classical perspective?

    A. Bureaucratic
    B. Scientific
    C. Quantitative
    D. Administrative

6. For the production of high-cost, low-volume products, the _____ layout is probably best.

    A. product
    B. fixed-position
    C. process
    D. conveyor

7. Which of the following is not a type of *responsibility center* that is used as a managerial control?

    A. Production center
    B. Profit center
    C. Revenue center
    D. Investment center

8. During the appraisal of an employee's performance, a human resources manager uses a general impression based on a few characteristics of the employee in order to judge other characteristics of the employee.
What type of rating error has occurred?

    A. Recency
    B. Severity
    C. Halo effect
    D. Contrast

9. As plans become more short-range, their

   A. function increases
   B. scope broadens
   C. specificity decreases
   D. specificity increases

10. According to Mintzberg's typology, an *adhocracy* is a management structural configuration that is characterized by each of the following EXCEPT

    A. high formalization
    B. various forms of matrix departmentalization
    C. expertise dispersed throughout
    D. emphasis on mutual adjustment

11. Each of the following is an advantage associated with low job discretion EXCEPT

    A. allowing management to establish performance standards
    B. encouraging innovation and creativity of employees
    C. reducing loss of time through consultation
    D. greater management control over work methods

12. In the management of human resources, the MAIN difference between replacement planning and succession planning is that

    A. replacement planning focuses on specific candidates who could fill designated managerial positions
    B. in replacement planning, age is used to track possible retirements
    C. succession planning focuses on specific candidates who could fill designated managerial positions
    D. in succession planning, age is used to track possible retirements

13. Of the following strategic role stages involved in operations management, which is performed FIRST?

    A. Support overall organizational strategy
    B. Achieve parity with competition
    C. Pursue operations management-based strategy
    D. Minimize negative potential

14. The top-down method of budgeting works particularly well in each of the following situations EXCEPT when

    A. unit managers have limited knowledge of the current situation
    B. the budgeting process must be expediently performed
    C. business needs necessitate close coordination among units
    D. there is an economic crisis

15. A company's _____ policy will decide the control and scheduling of production.

    A. financial
    B. personnel
    C. marketing
    D. product

16. Each of the following is an example of a carrying cost for raw materials EXCEPT

    A. spoilage costs
    B. taxes
    C. bid preparation time
    D. storage

17. Which of the following is a qualitative measure of goal achievement?   17.____

    A. Morale   B. Market share
    C. Gross income   D. Turnover

18. When production components are arranged according to the steps involved in producing   18.____
    a product, _____ layout occurs.

    A. fixed-position   B. input
    C. process   D. product

19. Technological change in a company's environment typically causes the company to   19.____
    develop

    A. control   B. recruitment
    C. marketing   D. monitoring

20. An MRP file is intended to control each of the following EXCEPT   20.____

    A. personnel requirements   B. priorities for materials
    C. inventory   D. capacity planning

21. The goal of management by objectives (MBO) is to stimulate better performance through   21.____
    _____ management.

    A. reactive   B. proactive
    C. authoritarian   D. synectic

22. In Vroom's expectancy theory, what is the term for the perceived relationship between   22.____
    effort and performance?

    A. Valence   B. Instrumentality
    C. Expectancy   D. Halo

23. The behavioral perspective on management includes   23.____

    A. the managerial importance of group dynamics
    B. the development of quantitative tools to assist in providing products and services
    C. the improvement of work methods through study
    D. identification of circumstances that will influence which particular approach will be effective in a given situation

24. _____ layout is the term for a production layout that groups similar work components   24.____
    and equipment.

    A. Fixed-position   B. Conveyor
    C. Product   D. Process

25. In organizational management, *span of control* refers to   25.____

    A. the number of people reporting to one manager
    B. formalized rules and procedures
    C. the separation of operating units
    D. the centralization of decision-making

KEY (CORRECT ANSWERS)

1. A
2. D
3. B
4. D
5. C
6. B
7. A
8. C
9. D
10. A

11. B
12. A
13. D
14. B
15. D
16. C
17. A
18. D
19. D
20. A

21. B
22. C
23. A
24. D
25. A

TEST 3

DIRECTIONS: Each question or incomplete statement is followed by several suggested answers or completions. Select the one that BEST answers the question or completes the statement. *PRINT THE LETTER OF THE CORRECT ANSWER IN THE SPACE AT THE RIGHT.*

1. When a manager's decision-making model is described as *incremental,* the manager('s)   1.____

    A. seeks alternatives only until a satisfactory solution is found
    B. approach is geared toward achieving short-term results
    C. is seeking an optimal decision
    D. is behaving in a random pattern, making nonprogrammed decisions

2. _____ is an example of task change.   2.____

    A. On-the-job training B. Automation
    C. Survey feedback D. Job enlargement

3. Which of the following is MOST likely to influence the complexity of a company's environment?   3.____

    A. Number of customers
    B. Amount of sophisticated knowledge available
    C. Size of the market
    D. Degree of government regulation

4. Each of the following is a stage involved in group development EXCEPT   4.____

    A. orientation B. growth
    C. cohesion D. evaluation

5. Which of the following is LEAST likely to be among the positive effects of the budgeting process?   5.____

    A. Encouraging innovative thinking to meet resource allocation
    B. Keeping managers informed about organizational activities
    C. Enhancing coordination across units
    D. Providing standards against which managers' performance can be evaluated

6. During the planning stage, a manager uses several years of historical data on sales to fit a line to predict future sales. This is an example of   6.____

    A. regression analysis B. time-series analysis
    C. causal modeling D. trend projection

7. When developing a management information system, a company is likely to implement system development during the _____ phase.   7.____

    A. testing B. operation
    C. integration D. planning

8. In production operations and control, quality control is a function of   8.____

    A. production design B. selection
    C. production planning D. production evaluation

21

9. A company decides to perform an internal social audit in which the company's social activities and resources and expenses used to participate are listed. After these numbers are compiled, the company assesses the extent to which it has reached its goals for each program.
   What type of assessment has been made?

   A. Cost approach
   B. Inventory approach
   C. Program management approach
   D. Cost-benefit analysis

10. In reinforcement theory, the successive rewarding of behaviors that closely approximate the desired response, until the actual desired response is made, is known as

   A. negative reinforcement
   B. shaping
   C. behavior modification
   D. extinction

11. A middle-level manager appoints a staff member to serve on a committee in the surrounding community. In terms of forming responses to social issues, the manager is practicing

   A. implicit change
   B. structural change
   C. tokenism
   D. functional change

12. The chain of command and problems of authority are issues of

   A. grouping
   B. coordination
   C. organizing
   D. influence

13. Which of the following is an example of reciprocal interdependence?

   A. Ordering and manufacturing
   B. Airline operations and maintenance
   C. A Dodge plant and a Plymouth plant
   D. Shipping and accounting

14. Each of the following is considered to be an element in a company's economic environment EXCEPT

   A. competitors
   B. investors
   C. suppliers
   D. demographic trends

15. A decision support system is a computer-based system that is used to

   A. execute and record day-to-day routine transactions
   B. aid the decision-making process in situations that are not well-structured
   C. automate certain office tasks
   D. allow on-line access to information needed by managers mainly at the middle and first-line levels

16. An operating budget that indicates anticipated revenues is the

   A. profit budget
   B. balance sheet
   C. sales budget
   D. cash budget

17. On an organization chart, a dotted line represents a

    A. vertically integrated distribution channel
    B. staff authority relationship
    C. horizontally integrated distribution channel
    D. direct authority relationship

18. Which dimension of quality involves supplements to the basic functioning characteristics of a product or service?

    A. Reliability
    B. Serviceability
    C. Performance
    D. Features

19. Each of the following is an advantage associated with conducting a social audit EXCEPT

    A. tangibility of results
    B. fostering a greater concern for social issues among organization members
    C. provision of data for comparing effectiveness of various programs
    D. illumination of areas in which the organization is vulnerable to public pressure

20. Which of the following types of management structures is most compatible with a stable environment?

    A. Matrix
    B. Functional
    C. Product
    D. Geographic

21. _____ characteristics are NOT a situational factor for a leader.

    A. Personality
    B. Managerial
    C. Subordinate
    D. Organizational

22. _____ is the term for the rules governing group behavior.

    A. Command modules
    B. Norms
    C. Functions
    D. Fronts

23. Of the following, top-down budgeting BEST incorporates

    A. information on competition
    B. alternative courses of action
    C. operational plans
    D. overall resource availability

24. Each of the following is likely to be a purpose of a company's strategic plan EXCEPT

    A. making future decisions
    B. generating options for consideration
    C. improving coordination of activities
    D. developing management

25. A stock of items that are currently being transformed into a final product or service is known as a(n) _____ inventory.

    A. input
    B. output
    C. work-in-process
    D. finished-goods

KEY (CORRECT ANSWERS)

1. B
2. D
3. B
4. C
5. A

6. D
7. A
8. D
9. C
10. B

11. C
12. D
13. B
14. D
15. B

16. C
17. B
18. D
19. A
20. B

21. A
22. B
23. D
24. A
25. D

EXAMINATION SECTION
TEST 1

DIRECTIONS: Each question or incomplete statement is followed by several suggested answers or completions. Select the one that BEST answers the question or completes the statement. *PRINT THE LETTER OF THE CORRECT ANSWER IN THE SPACE AT THE RIGHT.*

1. An environmental analysis serves as the basis for

    A. leading
    B. organizing
    C. controlling
    D. planning

2. Which of the following is an advantage associated with product job grouping?

    A. Achieving coordination of efforts
    B. Facilitating development of functional expertise
    C. Broadening managerial perspectives
    D. Eliminating cost duplication

3. Each of the following is an internal information source for a company EXCEPT

    A. sales data for previous year
    B. information on competitor's activities
    C. annual reports
    D. records of company performance

4. _____ is a control principle which suggests managers should be informed of a situation only if control data show a significant deviation from standards.

    A. Goal incongruence
    B. Management by exception
    C. Tactical control
    D. Management by objectives

5. On which of the following does an analysis of the internal environment direct its focus?

    A. Government regulations
    B. Demographic changes
    C. Organizational resources
    D. Availability of funds

6. A retail cosmetics store develops a plan for store expansion. What type of plan is being developed?

    A. Standing plan
    B. Budget
    C. Program
    D. Project

7. According to the path–goal theory of leadership, which of the following is one of the main functions of a leader?

    A. Redesigning work
    B. Motivation of subordinates
    C. Noninterference of subordinates
    D. Developing organizational goals

8. Each of the following is an advantage associated with the systems approach to management EXCEPT

   A. considering how an organization interacts with its environment
   B. providing a framework for assessing how well an organization's parts interact to achieve a common purpose
   C. emphasizing the diagnosis of problems within individual units
   D. used to analyze the organization at many levels

9. In a _____ environment, a problem-seeking style is most likely to succeed.

   A. predictable   B. simple
   C. dynamic   D. stable

10. An example of process technology is

    A. ship building   B. chemical manufacturing
    C. neurosurgery   D. textile manufacturing

11. According to _____ theory, an employee's behavior can be modified by changes in the external environment.

    A. cognitive   B. social learning
    C. reinforcement   D. self-actualization

12. Which of the following steps in deciding whether to expand or contract available facilities would be performed FIRST?

    A. Generating and evaluating alternatives
    B. Comparing current capacity with probable future demand
    C. Considering risks
    D. Using forecasts to determine probable future demand

13. Each of the following is considered to be a use of an organization chart EXCEPT

    A. communicating with people outside the organization
    B. showing informal working relationships
    C. showing intended reporting relationships between people
    D. illustrating where people are positioned in the structure

14. The Hawthorne studies of the 1920s and 1930s ultimately led to the _____ view of management.

    A. administrative   B. systems
    C. contingency   D. human relations

15. The settling of disputes over the interpretation of an agreement during collective bargaining is known as _____ arbitration.

    A. interest   B. verbal   C. rights   D. contract

16. The purpose of social scanning is to

    A. detect evidence of impending changes that will affect the organization's social responsibilities
    B. detect areas in which an organization is vulnerable to public pressure
    C. evaluate the social performance of the company
    D. evaluating the organizational importance of social trends

17. Which of the following is true when a company's replacement ratio is too low?

    A. There has been blocking of lower-level personnel.
    B. Insufficient weeding out has taken place.
    C. Replacement costs are too high.
    D. A shortage of capable managers exists.

18. What stage of group development deals with public communication programs?

    A. Evaluation and control
    B. Growth and productivity
    C. Orientation
    D. Internal problem-solving

19. According to situational leadership theory, the technique of *participating* is used when followers are

    A. able to take responsibility but are unwilling or too insecure to do so
    B. able and willing to take responsibility
    C. unable to take responsibility but are willing to do so
    D. unable and unwilling or too insecure to take responsibility for a given task

20. Which of the following are concerned with boundaries for decision-making and standing guidelines?

    A. Policies
    B. Procedures
    C. Rules
    D. Goals and strategies

21. Referent leader power

    A. results in a greater freedom to punish others
    B. relies on a possession of expertise that is admired by others
    C. generates greater control over information
    D. results from being admired or liked by others

22. Which of the following steps in the strategic planning process would be performed FIRST?

    A. Identifying the company's mission
    B. Setting the bottom line
    C. Developing a management succession plan
    D. Determining the capital equipment purchase plan for the coming year

23. A line worker checks the metal finish of new motorcycles. This is an example of _____ quality control.

    A. input
    B. feedforward
    C. feedback
    D. output

24. Which of the following is an example of *upward* communication?

    A. Suggestion boxes
    B. Bulletin boards
    C. Supervisory meetings
    D. Posters

25. Each of the following is considered a subordinate characteristic in the path–goal theory of leadership EXCEPT the employee's

    A. ability
    B. confidence
    C. needs
    D. task

KEY (CORRECT ANSWERS)

1.	D	11.	C
2.	A	12.	D
3.	B	13.	B
4.	B	14.	D
5.	C	15.	C
6.	C	16.	A
7.	B	17.	D
8.	C	18.	A
9.	C	19.	A
10.	B	20.	A

21. D
22. A
23. B
24. A
25. D

TEST 2

DIRECTIONS: Each question or incomplete statement is followed by several suggested answers or completions. Select the one that BEST answers the question or completes the statement. *PRINT THE LETTER OF THE CORRECT ANSWER IN THE SPACE AT THE RIGHT.*

1. A characteristic of an organic management system is 1.____

   A. centralized control
   B. nonprogrammed decision-making
   C. stable environment
   D. formal structure

2. A manager decides that three years of supervisory experience in the company qualifies an employee for promotion. What type of decision has the manager made? 2.____

   A. Conjunctive B. Subjunctive
   C. Disjunctive D. Compensatory

3. Charles Babbage's (1792–1871) contribution to management theory involved 3.____

   A. bureaucratic management B. cognitive theory
   C. work specialization D. management-as-science

4. What is the term for a data bank containing basic information about each employee that can be used to assess the likely availability of individuals for meeting current and future human resource needs? 4.____

   A. Job description B. Skills inventory
   C. Job specification D. Replacement chart

5. Each of the following would be a likely entry barrier into the iron ore industry EXCEPT 5.____

   A. track record B. technical knowledge
   C. tax laws D. capital equipment

6. What is the main DISADVANTAGE associated with the use of a behavioral model for decision-making in a company? 6.____

   A. Difficulty in perceiving existing problems
   B. The search for solutions is unlimited
   C. There is no assumption that decision makers evaluate their decisions against a set of organizational goals
   D. It is an abstraction that cannot fully describe actual decision-making behavior

7. If a matrix structure creates problems within an organization, they will *most likely* involve 7.____

   A. unity of command B. direction
   C. labor specialization D. morale

8. _____ power, if exercised by a manager, is most likely to result in the compliance of subordinates. 8.____

   A. Legitimate B. Expert
   C. Coercive D. Referent

9. An airline company decides to expand its route structure beyond its resource capability. The company has ignored the _____ criterion for strategic planning.

   A. internal consistency
   B. external consistency
   C. competitive advantage
   D. contribution to society

10. For a process layout, the MOST important factor for success is

    A. automation
    B. materials handling
    C. personnel training
    D. materials availability

11. Which of the following is LEAST likely to be a way in which managerial controls might create bureaucratic barriers to innovation?

    A. Focusing on short-term results
    B. Frequent, unpleasant surprises
    C. Use of accounting controls that assess all costs associated with a project in its early stage
    D. Excessive rationalism

12. Which of the following is a destructive force that is most likely to affect the initial problem-solving phase of the development of a quality circle?

    A. Disagreement on problems
    B. Savings not realized
    C. Lack of operations knowledge
    D. Resistance by implementation groups

13. Each of the following factors should be considered by a manager before deciding to fire a poorly performing employee EXCEPT

    A. family situation
    B. previous rewards
    C. satisfaction of job-related needs
    D. adequacy of job training

14. In an open job market,

    A. it is difficult for all candidates to find a job
    B. there are more jobs available than qualified candidates
    C. there are more qualified candidates than jobs available
    D. the number of jobs available and qualified candidates are roughly equal

15. The principle of _____ states that a job grouping arrangement can change at different levels of an organization.

    A. mutation
    B. effort
    C. alternation
    D. dispersion

16. According to Fiedler's theory, an employee-oriented style of leadership is most appropriate when there is _____ level of certainty.

    A. any
    B. a high
    C. a moderate
    D. a low

17. Corporate strategic plans should NOT be

   A. short-term
   B. original
   C. enlivening
   D. decisional

18. In order to effectively solve a technical problem facing a computer company that wants to enter the network computer market, a manager sends a questionnaire to various hardware experts throughout the country, soliciting their ideas about how to solve the problem.
   This is an example of

   A. outsourcing
   B. the Delphi technique
   C. nominal group technique
   D. linear programming

19. The use of a standard cost center is appropriate *only* if

   A. the unit has significant control over other expenses
   B. standards for costs involved in producing a product cannot be accurately estimated
   C. it is used to measure the direct profit impact of the unit's efforts
   D. the unit cannot be held directly responsible for profit levels

20. Which type of managerial power is NOT based on the control of important organizational resources?

   A. Information
   B. Reward
   C. Coercive
   D. Legitimate

21. A company performs an internal social audit in which the company's social activities over a given period of time are merely listed. What type of assessment has been made?

   A. Cost-benefit analysis
   B. Program management approach
   C. Cost approach
   D. Inventory approach

22. A stock of items that have been produced and are awaiting transit to a customer is a(n) _____ inventory.

   A. input
   B. work-in-process
   C. finished-goods
   D. feedforward

23. For _____, formal rules and procedures would be MOST effective.

   A. a research company
   B. a manufacturing company
   C. executive management
   D. test-marketing new products

24. Each of the following is an order cost for raw materials EXCEPT

   A. spoilage costs
   B. transportation expenses
   C. bid preparation expenses
   D. clerical expenses

25. A company's financial planning process typically includes each of the following EXCEPT 25.____
    A. predicting revenues
    B. budgeting
    C. forming separate planning staffs
    D. predicting costs

KEY (CORRECT ANSWERS)

1. B
2. C
3. C
4. B
5. C

6. D
7. A
8. A
9. A
10. B

11. B
12. C
13. A
14. B
15. C

16. C
17. A
18. B
19. D
20. A

21. D
22. C
23. B
24. A
25. C

TEST 3

DIRECTIONS: Each question or incomplete statement is followed by several suggested answers or completions. Select the one that BEST answers the question or completes the statement. *PRINT THE LETTER OF THE CORRECT ANSWER IN THE SPACE AT THE RIGHT.*

1. Which of the following factors favors centralization of computerized information system resources?

    A. Higher degree of user control
    B. Avoidance of project backlog
    C. Cost–effectiveness of smaller computers
    D. Enhanced staff professionalism

    1.____

2. Nonprogrammed decisions are MOST likely made by

    A. workers
    B. low–level management
    C. middle–level management
    D. executives

    2.____

3. Each of the following is a factor in human resource planning EXCEPT

    A. the actions of competitors
    B. organizational goals
    C. labor trends
    D. the legal environment

    3.____

4. Moving from _____ is an example of a radial career path.

    A. finance to marketing
    B. a line position to a staff position
    C. sales to management
    D. production to marketing

    4.____

5. _____ is a statistical technique that uses periodic random samples taken during production to determine whether acceptable quality levels are being met.

    A. AQL
    B. Statistical process control
    C. EOQ
    D. Acceptance sampling

    5.____

6. A company's ability to meet its maturing financial obligations is known as its _____ ratio.

    A. profitability
    B. liquidity
    C. leverage
    D. operating

    6.____

7. Which of the following is a DISADVANTAGE associated with the use of external recruitment in the management of human resources?

    A. Fewer new ideas introduced into the company
    B. Susceptibility of selection to office politics
    C. Frequent necessity for extensive training
    D. Higher costs than internal recruitment

    7.____

8. A company's management sets a goal defined as decreasing customer complaints. What type of goal has been set for the company?

   A. Operational
   B. Resource
   C. Developmental
   D. Improvement

9. Each of the following is a type of inventory EXCEPT

   A. in–process
   B. raw materials
   C. subassemblies
   D. finished products

10. Which of the following was NOT involved in developing the scientific approach to management?

    A. Babbage
    B. Gantt
    C. Taylor
    D. Gilbreth

11. The decision to introduce a new product line is a(n) _____ decision.

    A. programmed
    B. nonprogrammed
    C. detail
    D. under certainty

12. A statistical analysis of a company's present employees is termed

    A. replacement chart
    B. human resources audit
    C. performance ratio
    D. staffing analysis

13. Medium–range capacity planning

    A. is typically made only by top management
    B. is aimed at ensuring that the capacities of the current major facilities are being utilized effectively within the context of the master production schedule
    C. is more likely to make use of capacity requirements planning than other methods
    D. provides information on possible means of making limited adjustments in capacity

14. Which of the following is NOT an element of a company's internal environment?

    A. Competitors
    B. Personnel
    C. Budgeting
    D. Working capital

15. The degree to which individuals can plan and control the work involved in their jobs is known as

    A. task identity
    B. job depth
    C. job enrichment
    D. job scope

16. The bottom–up method of budgeting works particularly well when

    A. unit managers have limited knowledge of the current situation
    B. first–line management is excluded from the process
    C. competitive pressures require a quick response
    D. there is a considerable degree of interdependence among units

17. What type of control is illustrated by production quality control?

    A. Screening   B. Process   C. Input   D. Output

18. As they are widely practiced, what is the main DISADVANTAGE associated with interviews as a means of job selection?

    A. Does not allow preliminary consideration
    B. Formality
    C. Adverse impact
    D. Low validity of information

19. _____ technology involves the highest demands for communication.

    A. Long–linked   B. Intensive
    C. Long–term   D. Mediating

20. Typically, which of the following steps in the budgetary process would occur LAST?

    A. Unit manager formulates performance targets.
    B. Top management outlines resource restraints.
    C. Top management combines unit budgets.
    D. Unit managers plan activities in detail.

21. Each of the following is typically a feature of a collective bargaining agreement EXCEPT

    A. union security clause
    B. rules for selection of arbitrators
    C. grievance procedures
    D. employment–at–will provision

22. Managers at the lowest level of management who are directly responsible for the work of operating employees are known as _____ managers.

    A. functional level   B. general
    C. first–line   D. operative

23. _____ is a condition in which individuals engage in behaviors that are encouraged by controls and related reward systems, even though the behaviors are actually inconsistent with organizational goals.

    A. Role conflict   B. Extinction
    C. Negative reinforcement D. Behavioral displacement

24. _____ data is a characteristic of the preceptive style of information–gathering.

    A. Expanding   B. Filtering
    C. Anticipating   D. Processing all

25. Which of the following is a characteristic of a bureaucratic organization?

    A. Stability   B. Uncertainty
    C. Flexibility   D. Dynamic structure

KEY (CORRECT ANSWERS)

1. D
2. D
3. A
4. B
5. B

6. B
7. D
8. D
9. C
10. A

11. B
12. B
13. D
14. A
15. B

16. C
17. B
18. D
19. B
20. C

21. D
22. C
23. D
24. B
25. A

EXAMINATION SECTION
TEST 1

DIRECTIONS: Each question or incomplete statement is followed by several suggested answers or completions. Select the one that BEST answers the question or completes the statement. *PRINT THE LETTER OF THE CORRECT ANSWER IN THE SPACE AT THE RIGHT.*

1. What type of reinforcement schedule is illustrated by a sales commission? 1._____
   - A. Variable interval
   - B. Variable ratio
   - C. Fixed interval
   - D. Fixed ratio

2. Mathematical models of management grew out of the _____ school of management. 2._____
   - A. behavioral
   - B. systems
   - C. contingency
   - D. scientific

3. *Individual equity* is the term for the extent to which 3._____
   - A. pay rates allocated to specific individuals within the organization reflect variations in individual merit
   - B. pay rates for particular jobs correspond to rates paid for similar jobs on the entire job market
   - C. pay rates for various jobs inside the organization reflect the relative worth of those jobs
   - D. compensable factors will be used to rate the worth of particular jobs

4. External audits of a company are normally performed every 4._____
   - A. month
   - B. quarter
   - C. year
   - D. two years

5. Production design is primarily concerned with _____ controls. 5._____
   - A. marginal
   - B. process
   - C. input
   - D. output

6. The use of profit centers is appropriate only when 6._____
   - A. it is used to measure the direct profit impact of the unit's efforts
   - B. the unit is responsible for revenues, but does not have control over costs of the products they handle
   - C. the unit has significant control over both costs and revenues
   - D. the unit has control over investment decisions

7. A human resource manager's attention should be focused *primarily* on _____ during managerial selection. 7._____
   - A. job behavior
   - B. education level
   - C. interview results
   - D. test scores

8. Which of the following computer-based information systems would be used to handle word processing? 8._____
   - A. TPS
   - B. MIS
   - C. OAS
   - D. DSS

9. The technique most useful for solving inventory problems is

   A. the Delphi technique B. EOQ
   C. queuing D. linear programming

10. A commission formed by a company is responsible to

    A. the general public B. top-level management
    C. union leaders D. stockholders

11. Each of the following is typically considered an ordering cost EXCEPT

    A. time B. paperwork
    C. pilferage D. postage

12. The use of scenarios may help managers to

    A. tighten day-to-day control
    B. examine different possible outcomes
    C. lengthen their reaction times
    D. anticipate the unknowable

13. During the appraisal of an employee's performance, a human resources manager tends to compare the employee with other coworkers, rather than with a performance standard. What type of rating error is occurring?

    A. Severity error B. Contrast error
    C. Halo effect D. Recency error

14. A supervisor rates a subordinate's initiative in an evaluation. This is an example of a(n) _____ measure.

    A. cognitive B. emotional
    C. qualitative D. quantitative

15. A _____ budget is NOT an operating budget.

    A. profit B. cash C. expense D. sales

16. Which of the following is a characteristic of a dynamic, complex company environment?

    A. Predictability
    B. Minimal need of sophisticated knowledge
    C. Numerous products and services
    D. Stability

17. A management information system is capable of each of the following EXCEPT

    A. making unprogrammed decisions
    B. providing early warning signals
    C. aiding decision-making
    D. automating clerical functions

18. In reinforcement theory, a technique that involves withholding previously available positive consequences associated with a behavior, in order to *decrease* that behavior, is known as

    A. negative reinforcement
    B. shaping
    C. punishment
    D. extinction

19. Which of the following is NOT a disadvantage associated with highly specialized, low-discretion jobs?

    A. Failing to utilize employee intelligence
    B. Can result in unproductive behaviors
    C. Requiring hiring highly trained, more expensive labor
    D. Is inconsistent with values and lifestyles of employees

20. Which of the following is an example of a line department?

    A. Production
    B. Finance
    C. Accounting
    D. Research and development

21. A computer-based OAS system is intended *primarily* to

    A. execute routine transactions
    B. allow access to historic information
    C. improve the decision-making process
    D. facilitate communication

22. The process of acquainting new employees with the policies and standards of the company is known as

    A. recruitment
    B. orientation
    C. staffing
    D. development

23. What is the term for the process of planning how to match supply with product or service demand over a time horizon of approximately one year?

    A. Capacity planning
    B. Forecasting
    C. Aggregate production planning
    D. Capacity requirements planning

24. Authority is correctly defined as the

    A. right to command and allocate resources
    B. accountability for achievement of goals and the efficient use of resources
    C. ability to influence others and control resources
    D. tendency to delegate tasks

25. According to situational leadership theory, when subordinates are able and willing to take appropriate responsibility, the appropriate leadership action is

    A. telling
    B. selling
    C. delegating
    D. participating

KEY (CORRECT ANSWERS)

1. D
2. D
3. A
4. C
5. C

6. C
7. A
8. C
9. B
10. A

11. C
12. B
13. B
14. C
15. B

16. C
17. A
18. D
19. C
20. A

21. D
22. B
23. C
24. A
25. C

TEST 2

DIRECTIONS: Each question or incomplete statement is followed by several suggested answers or completions. Select the one that BEST answers the question or completes the statement. *PRINT THE LETTER OF THE CORRECT ANSWER IN THE SPACE AT THE RIGHT.*

1. Formalized job rotation programs are an example of

    A. training
    B. career pathing
    C. recruitment
    D. career counseling

    1._____

2. A(n) _____ is an example of a process layout pattern.

    A. automobile assembly line
    B. food processing plant
    C. department store
    D. hospital

    2._____

3. Which of the following is MOST likely to be an output from a computerized decision support system?

    A. Projections
    B. Summary reports
    C. Special reports
    D. Schedules

    3._____

4. When a company's replacement ratio is too high,

    A. replacement costs are too high
    B. there has been blocking of lower–level personnel
    C. insufficient weeding out has taken place
    D. a shortage of capable managers exists

    4._____

5. An advantage associated with functional job grouping is that it

    A. facilitates organizational growth
    B. allows for easier hiring
    C. makes allocation of expenses easier
    D. facilitates coordination of top managers

    5._____

6. Which of the following is an advantage associated with group decision–making?

    A. Choice of best alternative
    B. Less time–consuming
    C. Encouragement of innovative thinking
    D. Lower cost

    6._____

7. On an organization chart, a solid line represents a(n)

    A. vertically integrated distribution channel
    B. indirect authority relationship
    C. horizontally integrated distribution channel
    D. line authority relationship

    7._____

8. Which type of power, if exercised by a manager, is most likely to secure the commitment of subordinates?

    A. Legitimate
    B. Reward
    C. Information
    D. Referent

    8._____

41

9. Which functional area of a company involves employee relations?

   A. Finance
   B. Marketing
   C. Operations
   D. Development

10. In a restaurant, a manager tallies the number of meals that are served within 15 minutes of the customer orders. Which type of statistical quality control measure is the manager using?

   A. Input   B. Marginal   C. Attribute   D. Variable

11. Low-level analysis is most likely to be processed by which of the following kinds of computer information systems?

   A. TPS   B. DSS   C. OAS   D. MIS

12. Of the following, bottom-up budgeting best incorporates

   A. information on markets
   B. company planning parameters
   C. corporate goals
   D. industry projections

13. A worker experiences role _____ when his/her role within the organization is unclear.

   A. discord
   B. confusion
   C. ambiguity
   D. conflict

14. Which of the following is a DISADVANTAGE associated with the use of pay as an enforcer of employee performance?

   A. Time lag
   B. Low employee value
   C. Unequal pay among employees
   D. Erosion of value due to inflation

15. A company forms a temporary task force to study a problem in the community, and the company's relationship to that problem. In terms of forming responses to social issues, the company is practicing

   A. implicit change
   B. structural change
   C. tokenism
   D. functional change

16. A manager cannot assign probabilities to outcomes because he lacks information. The manager is said to be making a decision under the condition of

   A. peril
   B. certainty
   C. uncertainty
   D. risk

17. Using the resource dependence approach to controls, a manager determines that her unit is highly dependent on another unit for a particular resource, and that the expected resource flows are unacceptable. It is also determined, however, that the control process is probably not feasible for her department.
The manager should

   A. do nothing
   B. research a way to lower costs
   C. develop alternatives to control
   D. initiate the control process and try to adjust as it progresses

18. In the path–goal theory of leadership, the monitoring and control aspects of a leader's behavior are examples of _____ behavior.

   A. participative   B. supportive
   C. instrumental   D. goal–oriented

19. When a particular task is simple and morale is not an issue, _____ communication is probably the best method.

   A. circle   B. chain
   C. wheel   D. all–channel

20. In production and operations control, establishing a wage and salary structure is a function of

   A. production planning   B. production design
   C. production evaluation D. selection

21. Which of the following is a type of inventory that consists of raw materials, components, and subassemblies that are used in the production of an end product or service?

   A. Dependent demand inventory
   B. Bill of materials
   C. Independent demand inventory
   D. Cost inventory

22. _____ job testing is a means of measuring mainly mental, mechanical, and clerical capacities.

   A. Personality   B. Ability
   C. Performance   D. Replacement

23. Historically, the management theory that first emphasized the need for companies to operate in a rational manner rather than according to the whims of owners and managers was the theory of _____ management.

   A. behaviorist   B. quantitative
   C. administrative   D. bureaucratic

24. Which of the following is an example of *discretionary* costs?

   A. Raw materials   B. Mortgages
   C. Sales commissions   D. Accounting fees

25. According to the systems approach to management, a system that operates in continual interaction with its environment is a(n) _____ system.

    A. open   B. feedback   C. charged   D. looped

KEY (CORRECT ANSWERS)

1.	A	11.	D
2.	C	12.	A
3.	C	13.	C
4.	B	14.	A
5.	B	15.	D
6.	A	16.	C
7.	D	17.	C
8.	D	18.	C
9.	C	19.	C
10.	C	20.	B

21. A
22. B
23. D
24. D
25. A

TEST 3

DIRECTIONS: Each question or incomplete statement is followed by several suggested answers or completions. Select the one that BEST answers the question or completes the statement. *PRINT THE LETTER OF THE CORRECT ANSWER IN THE SPACE AT THE RIGHT.*

1. In a complex organization, the process of differentiation is likely to create problems associated with 1.____

    A. controlling size
    B. management training
    C. coordination
    D. motivation

2. Before a company can determine whether a management information system can be developed, a(n) _____ must be performed. 2.____

    A. algorithm
    B. organizational chart
    C. feasibility study
    D. conversion

3. Job testing is considered to be reliable when 3.____

    A. a good test score is a clear predictor of job success
    B. the test measures what it professes to measure
    C. the test is clearly related to the job
    D. the candidate would earn roughly the same score if the test were repeated

4. A control system that is self–regulating is said to be 4.____

    A. formalized
    B. feedback–looped
    C. cybernetic
    D. centralized

5. A company with many rules and procedures is usually described as having a(n) _____ span of control. 5.____

    A. almost nonexistent
    B. narrow
    C. moderate
    D. wide

6. Altogether, the various types of financial statements are considered _____ control. 6.____

    A. input   B. output   C. process   D. steering

7. A human resources manager teaches a new employee what to do, where to go for help, and what the company's important rules and policies are. What stage of orientation is being transacted? 7.____

    A. Implementation
    B. Socialization
    C. Induction
    D. Evaluation

8. The factors necessary in order to estimate partial–factor productivity are _____ and goods/services produced. 8.____

    A. labor hours
    B. labor hours, capital,
    C. capital, energy, materials,
    D. labor hours, capital, energy, technology, materials,

9. A company's _____ policy will decide the channels of distribution for a given product. 9.____

    A. financial
    B. personnel
    C. marketing
    D. product

45

10. Which of the following factors favors decentralization of computerized information system resources?

    A. Increasing availability of user-friendly software
    B. Staff specialization
    C. Easier control of corporate databases
    D. Potential for economies of scale

11. Each of the following typically helps implement authority in an organization EXCEPT

    A. span of control
    B. centralization
    C. chain of command
    D. familiarity

12. A maintenance goal

    A. implies a specific level of activity over time
    B. expresses the hope for growth
    C. uses action verbs to indicate change
    D. implies an effort to reorganize

13. Each of the following is a potential pitfall associated with financial controls EXCEPT

    A. neglecting to link controls to strategic planning process
    B. stifling innovation and creativity
    C. not sophisticated enough for organizational needs
    D. mixed messages about desired behaviors

14. The term for a statement of the skills, abilities, education, and previous work experience required to perform a particular job is the

    A. replacement chart
    B. job specification
    C. job description
    D. job analysis

15. The most successful use of the practice of job rotation is

    A. to create maximum flexibility through cross-training
    B. as an employee development tool
    C. to alleviate boredom with simple jobs
    D. to improve departmental loyalty

16. A company vice president delegates the authority to make a decision to a product manager. This is an example of

    A. outsourcing
    B. horizontal decentralization
    C. vertical decentralization
    D. centralized decision-making

17. Time-and-motion studies were first carried out by the _____ school of management.

    A. scientific
    B. human relations
    C. classical
    D. contingency

18. What is the term for the dispersion of organizational power?

    A. Unity of command
    B. Span of control
    C. Formalization
    D. Decentralization

19. _____ is the term for a technique to enhance creativity that relies on analogies.

    A. Storming
    B. Entropy
    C. Cybernetics
    D. Synectics

20. Which of the following is NOT considered to be a limitation associated with organization charts?

    A. May not indicate real power and influence of people on the chart
    B. Does not show a picture of the structure at a particular point in time
    C. Frequently outdated
    D. May not show actual formal relationships

21. Which of the following is considered to be a *snapshot* of an organization at a particular point in time?

    A. Expense budget
    B. Income statement
    C. Balance sheet
    D. Cash flow statement

22. Each of the following would be considered a safety and security need for an employee EXCEPT

    A. merit pay raises
    B. job security
    C. pay raises references to the cost of living
    D. benefits

23. The behavioral model of management contributed the idea of

    A. quantitative aids for decision–making
    B. organization members as active human resources
    C. the potential importance of the environment to organizational success
    D. the need for a scientific approach to management

24. According to the contingency perspective, which of the following would NOT be a major contingency factor for a business?

    A. Strategy
    B. Size
    C. External environment
    D. Technology in use

25. Which of the following is NOT an example of a single–use plan?

    A. Standing plan
    B. Budget
    C. Project
    D. Program

KEY (CORRECT ANSWERS)

1.	B	11.	D
2.	C	12.	A
3.	D	13.	C
4.	C	14.	B
5.	D	15.	B
6.	B	16.	C
7.	C	17.	C
8.	A	18.	D
9.	C	19.	D
10.	A	20.	B

21. C
22. A
23. B
24. B
25. A

SUPERVISION, ADMINISTRATION, MANAGEMENT, AND ORGANIZATION
EXAMINATION SECTION
TEST 1

DIRECTIONS: Each question or incomplete statement is followed by several suggested answers or completions. Select the one that BEST answers the question or completes the statement. *PRINT THE LETTER OF THE CORRECT ANSWER IN THE SPACE AT THE RIGHT.*

1. In coaching a subordinate on the nature of decision-making, an executive would be right if he stated that the one of the following which is general the BEST definition of decision-making is:
   A. Choosing between alternatives
   B. Making diagnoses of feasible ends
   C. Making diagnoses of feasible means
   D. Comparing alternatives

2. Of the following, which one would be LEAST valid as a purpose of an organizational policy statement?
   To
   A. keep personnel from performing improper actions and functions on routine matters
   B. prevent the mishandling of non-routine matters
   C. provide management personnel with a tool that precludes the need for their use of judgment
   D. provide standard decisions and approaches in handling problems of a recurrent nature

3. Much has been written criticizing bureaucratic organizations. Current thinking on the subject is GENERALLY that
   A. bureaucracy is on the way out
   B. bureaucracy, though not perfect, is unlikely to be replaced
   C. bureaucratic organizations are most effective in dealing with constant change
   D. bureaucratic organizations are most effective when dealing with sophisticated customers or clients

4. The development of alternate plans as a major step in planning will normally result in the planner having several possible courses of action available. GENERALLY, this is
   A. *desirable*, since such development helps to determine the most suitable alternative and to provide for the unexpected
   B. *desirable*, since such development makes the use of planning premises and constraints unnecessary

C. *undesirable*, since the planners should formulate only one way of achieving given goals at a given time
D. *undesirable*, since such action restricts efforts to modify the planning to take advantage of opportunities

5. The technique of departmentation by task force includes the assigning of a team or task force to a definite project or block of work which extends from the beginning to the completing of a wanted and definite type and quantity of work. Of the following, the MOST important actor aiding the successful use of this technique *normally* is
   A. having the task force relatively large, at least one hundred members
   B. having a definite project termination date established
   C. telling each task force member what his next assignment will be only after the current project ends
   D. utilizing it only for projects that are regularly recurring

6. With respect to communication in small group settings such as may occur in business, government, and the military, it is generally TRUE that people usually derive more satisfaction and are usually more productive under conditions which
   A. permit communication only with superiors
   B. permit the minimum intragroup communication possible
   C. are generally restricted by management
   D. allow open communication among all group members

7. If an executive were asked to list some outstanding features of decentralization, which one of the following would NOT be such a feature?
   Decentralization
   A. provides decision-making experience for lower level managers
   B. promotes uniformity of policy
   C. is a relatively new concept in management
   D. is similar to the belief in encouragement of free enterprise

8. Modern management experts have emphasized the importance of the informal organization in motivating employees to increase productivity.
   Of the following, the characteristic which would have the MOST direct influence on employee motivation is the tendency of members of the informal organization to
   A. resist change
   B. establish their own norms
   C. have similar outside interests
   D. set substantially higher goals than those of management

9. According to leading management experts, the decision-making process contains separate and distinct steps that must be taken in an orderly sequence.
   Of the following arrangements, which one is in CORRECT order?

A. I. Search for alternatives; II. diagnosis; III. comparison; IV. choice
B. I. Diagnose; II. comparison; III. search for alternatives; IV. choice
C. I. Diagnose; II. search for alternatives; III. comparison; IV. choice
D. I. Diagnose; II. search for alternatives; III. choice; IV. comparison

10. Of the following, the growth of professionalism in large organizations can PRIMARILY be expected to result in
    A. greater equalization of power
    B. increased authoritarianism
    C. greater organizational disloyalty
    D. increased promotion opportunities

11. Assume an executive carries out his responsibilities to his staff according to what is now known about managerial leadership.
    Which of the following statements would MOST accurately reflect his assumptions about proper management?
    A. Efficiency in operations results from allowing the human element to participate in a minimal way.
    B. Efficient operation result from balancing work considerations with personnel considerations.
    C. Efficient operation results from a workforce committed to its self-interest.
    D. Efficient operation results from staff relationships that produce a friendly work climate.

12. Assume that an executive is called upon to conduct a management audit. To do this properly, he would have to take certain steps in a specific sequence.
    Of the following steps, which step should this manager take FIRST?
    A. Managerial performance must be surveyed.
    B. A method of reporting must be established.
    C. Management auditing procedures and documentation must be developed.
    D. Criteria for the audit must be considered.

13. If a manager is required to conduct a scientific investigation of an organizational problem, the FIRST step he should take is to
    A. state his assumptions about the problem
    B. carry out a search for background information
    C. choose the right approach to investigate the validity of his assumptions
    D. define and state the problem

14. An executive would be right to assert that the principle of delegation states that decisions should be made PRIMARILY
    A. by persons in an executive capacity qualified to make them
    B. by persons in a non-executive capacity
    C. at as low an organization level of authority as practicable
    D. by the next lower level of authority

15. Of the following, which one is NOT regarded by management authorities as a FUNDAMENTAL characteristic of an *ideal* bureaucracy?
    A. Division of labor and specialization
    B. An established hierarchy
    C. Decentralization of authority
    D. A set of operating rules and regulations

16. As the number of subordinates in a manager's span of control increases, the ACTUAL number of possible relationships
    A. increases disproportionately to the number of subordinates
    B. increases in equal number to the number of subordinates
    C. reaches a stable level
    D. will first increase then slowly decrease

17. An executive's approach to controlling the activities of his subordinates concentrated on ends rather than means, and was diagnostic rather than punitive.
    This manager may MOST properly be characterized as using the managerial technique of management-by-
    A. exception   B. objectives   C. crisis   D. default

18. In conducting a training session on the administrative control process, which of the following statements would be LEAST valid for an executive to make?
    Controlling
    A. requires checking upon assignments to see what is being done
    B. involves comparing what is being done to what ought to be done
    C. requires corrective action when what is being done does not meet expectations
    D. occurs after all the other managerial processes have been performed

19. The "brainstorming" technique for creative solutions of management problems MOST generally consists of
    A. bringing staff together in an exchange of a quantity of freewheeling ideas
    B. isolating individual staff members to encourage thought
    C. developing improved office procedures
    D. preparation of written reports on complex problems

20. Computer systems hardware MOST often operates in relation to which one of the following steps in solving a data-processing problem?
    A. Determining the problem
    B. Defining and stating the problem
    C. Implementing the programmed solution
    D. Completing the documentation of every unexplored solution

21. There is a tendency in management to upgrade objectives.
    This trend is generally regarded as
    A. *desirable*; the urge to improve is demonstrated by adopting objectives that have been adjusted to provide improved service

B. *undesirable*; the typical manager searches for problems which obstruct his objectives
C. *desirable*; it is common for a manager to find that the details of an immediate operation have occupied so much of his time that he has lost sight of the basic overall objective
D. *undesirable*; efforts are wasted when they are expended on a mass of uncertain objectives, since the primary need of most organizations is a single target or several major ones

22. Of the following, it is generally LEAST effective for an executive to delegate authority where working conditions involve
    A. rules establishing normal operating procedures
    B. consistent methods of operation
    C. rapidly changing work standards
    D. complex technology

23. If an executive was explaining the difficulty of making decisions under *risk* conditions, he would be MOST accurate if he said that such decisions would be difficult to make when the decision maker has _____ information and experience and can expect _____ outcomes for each action.
    A. limited; many
    B. much; many
    C. much; few
    D. limited; few

24. If an executive were asked to list some outstanding features of centralized organization, which one of the following would be INCORRECT?
    Centralized organization
    A. lessens risks of errors by unskilled subordinates
    B. utilizes the skills of specialized experts at a central location
    C. produces uniformity of policy and non-uniformity of action
    D. enables closer control of operations than a decentralized set-up

25. It is possible for an organization's management to test whether or not the organization has a sound structure.
    Of the following, which one is NOT a test of soundness in an organization's structure?
    The
    A. ability to replace key personnel with minimum loss of effectiveness
    B. ability of information and decisions to flow more freely through the *grapevine* than through formal channels
    C. provision for orderly organizational growth with the ability to handle change as the need arises.

KEY (CORRECT ANSWERS)

1. A
2. C
3. B
4. A
5. B

6. D
7. B
8. B
9. C
10. A

11. B
12. D
13. D
14. C
15. C

16. A
17. B
18. D
19. A
20. C

21. A
22. C
23. A
24. C
25. B

TEST 2

DIRECTIONS: Each question or incomplete statement is followed by several suggested answers or completions. Select the one that BEST answers the question or completes the statement. *PRINT THE LETTER OF THE CORRECT ANSWER IN THE SPACE AT THE RIGHT.*

1. Management experts generally believe that computer-based management information systems (MIS) have greater potential for improving the process of management than any other development in recent decades.
   The one of the following which MOST accurately describes the objectives of MIS is to
   A. provide information for decision-making on planning, initiating, and controlling the operations of the various units of the organization
   B. establish mechanization of routine functions such as clerical records, payroll, inventory, and accounts receivable in order to promote economy and efficiency
   C. computerize decision-making on planning, initiative, organizing, and controlling the operations of an organization
   D. provide accurate facts and figures on the various programs of the organization to be used for purposes of planning and research

   1.____

2. The one of the following which is the BEST application on the *management-by-exception* principle is that this principle
   A. stimulates communication and aids in management of crisis situations, thus reducing the frequency of decision-making
   B. saves time and reserves top-management decisions only for crisis situations, thus reducing the frequency of decision-making
   C. stimulates communication, saves time, and reduces the frequency of decision-making
   D. is limited to crisis-management situations

   2.____

3. It is generally recognized that each organization is dependent upon availability of qualified personnel.
   Of the following, the MOST important factor affecting the availability of qualified people to each organization is
   A. innovations in technology and science
   B. the general decline in the educational levels of our population
   C. the rise of sentiment against racial discrimination
   D. pressure by organized community groups

   3.____

4. A fundamental responsibility of all managers is to decide what physical facilities and equipment are needed to help attain basic goals.
   Good planning for the purchase and use of equipment is seldom easy to do and is complicated MOST by the fact that
   A. organizations rarely have stable sources of supply
   B. nearly all managers tend to be better at personnel planning than at equipment planning

   4.____

55

C. decisions concerning physical resources are made too often on a *crash basis* rather than under carefully prepared policies
D. legal rulings relative to depreciation fluctuate very frequently

5. In attempting to reconcile managerial objectives and an individual employee's goals, it is generally LEAST desirable for management to
   A. recognize the capacity of the individual to contribute toward realization of managerial goals
   B. encourage self-development of the employee to exceed minimum job performance
   C. consider an individual employee's work separately from other employees
   D. demonstrate that an employee advances only to the extent that he contributes directly to the accomplishment of stated goals

6. As a management tool for discovering individual training needs a job analysis would generally be of LEAST assistance in determining
   A. the performance requirements of individual jobs
   B. actual employee performance on the job
   C. acceptable standards of performance
   D. training needs for individual jobs

7. One of the major concerns of organizational managers today is how the spread of automation will affect them and the status of their positions. Realistically speaking, one can say that the MOST likely effect of our newer forms of highly automated technology on managers will be to
   A. make most top-level positions superfluous or obsolete
   B. reduce the importance of managerial work in general
   C. replace the work of managers with the work of technicians
   D. increase the importance of and demand for top managerial personnel

8. Which one of the following is LEAST likely to be an area or cause of trouble in the use of staff people (e.g., assistants to the administrator)?
   A. Misunderstanding of the role the staff people are supposed to play, as a result of vagueness of definition of their duties and authority
   B. Tendency of staff personnel almost always to be older than line personnel at comparable salary levels with who they must deal
   C. Selection of staff personnel who fail to have simultaneously both competence in their specialties and skill in staff work
   D. The staff person fails to understand mixed staff and operating duties

9. The one of the following which is the BEST measure of decentralization in an agency is the
   A. amount of checking required on decisions made at lower levels in the chain of command
   B. amount of checking required on decisions made at lower levels of the chain of command and the number of functions affected thereby
   C. number of functions affected by decisions made at higher levels
   D. number of functions affected by middle echelon decision-making

10. Which of the following is generally NOT a valid statement with respect to the supervisory process?
    A. General supervision is more effective than close supervision.
    B. Employee-centered supervisors lead more effectively than do production-centered supervisors.
    C. Employee satisfaction is directly related to productivity.
    D. Low-producing supervisors use techniques that are different from high-producing supervisors.

11. The one of the following which is the MOST essential element for proper evaluation of the performance of subordinate supervisors is a
    A. careful definition of each supervisor's specific job responsibilities and of his progress in meeting mutually agreed upon work goals
    B. system of rewards and penalties based on each supervisor's progress in meeting clearly defined performance standards
    C. definition of personality traits, such as industry, initiative, dependability, and cooperativeness, required for effective job performance
    D. breakdown of each supervisor's job into separate components and a rating of his performance on each individual task

12. The one of the following which is the PRINCIPAL advantage of specialization for the operating efficiency of a public service agency is that specialization
    A. reduces the amount of red tape in coordinating the activities of mutually dependent departments
    B. simplifies the problem of developing adequate job controls
    C. provides employees with a clear understanding of the relationship of their activities to the overall objectives of the agency
    D. reduces destructive competition for power between departments

13. Of the following, the group which generally benefits MOST from supervisory training programs in public service agencies are those supervisors who have
    A. accumulated a long period of total service to the agency
    B. responsibility for a large number of subordinate personnel
    C. been in the supervisory ranks for a long period of time
    D. a high level of formalized academic training

14. A list of conditions which encourages good morale inside a work group would NOT include a
    A. high rate of agreement among group members on values and objectives
    B. tight control system to minimize the risk of individual error
    C. good possibility that joint action will accomplish goals
    D. past history of successful group accomplishment

15. Of the following, the MOST important factor to be considered in selecting a training strategy or program is the
    A. requirements of the job to be performed by the trainees
    B. educational level or prior training of the trainees
    C. size of the training group
    D. quality and competence of available training specialists

16. Of the following, the one which is considered to be LEAST characteristic of the higher ranks of management is
    A. that higher levels of management benefit from modern technology
    B. that success is measured by the extent to which objectives are achieved
    C. the number of subordinates that directly report to an executive
    D. the de-emphasis of individual and specialized performance

17. Assume that an executive is preparing a training syllabus to be used in training members of his staff.
    Which of the following would NOT be a valid principle of the learning process for this manager to keep in mind in the preparation of the training syllabus?
    A. When a person has thoroughly learned a task, it takes a lot of effort to create a little more improvement.
    B. In complicated learning situations, there is a period in which an additional period of practice produces an equal amount of improvement in learning.
    C. The less a person knows about the task, the slower the initial progress.
    D. The more the person knows about the risk, the slower the initial progress.

18. Of the following, which statement BEST illustrates when collective bargaining agreements are working well?
    A. Executives strongly support subordinate managers.
    B. The management rights clause in the contract is clear and enforced.
    C. Contract provisions are competently interpreted.
    D. The provisions of the agreement are properly interpreted, communicated, and observed.

19. An executive who wishes to encourage subordinates to communicate freely with him about a job-related problem should FIRST
    A. state his own position on the problem before listening to the subordinates' ideas
    B. invite subordinates to give their own opinions on the problem
    C. ask subordinates for their reactions to his own ideas about the problem
    D. guard the confidentiality of management information about the problem

20. The ability to deal constructively with intra-organizational conflict is an essential attribute of the successful manager.
    The one of the following types of conflict which would be LEAST difficult to handle constructively is a situation in which there is
    A. agreement on objectives, but disagreement as to the probable results of adopting the various alternatives
    B. agreement on objectives, disagreement on alternative courses of action, and relative certainty as to the outcome of one of the alternatives
    C. disagreement on objectives and on alternate courses of action, but relative certainty as to the outcome of the alternatives
    D. disagreement on objectives and on alternative course of action, but uncertainty as to the outcome of the alternatives

21. Which of the following statements is LEAST accurate in describing formal job evaluation and wage and salary classification plans?
    A. Parties that disagree on wage matters can examine an established system rather than unsupported opinions.
    B. The use of such plans tends to overlook the effect of age and seniority of employees on job values in the plan.
    C. Such plans can eliminate salary controversies in organizations designing and using them properly.
    D. These plans are not particularly useful in checking on executive compensation.

22. In carrying out disciplinary action, the MOST important procedure for all managers to follow is to
    A. sell all levels of management on the need for discipline from the organization's viewpoint
    B. follow up on a disciplinary action and not assume that the action has been effective
    C. convince all executives that proper discipline is a legitimate tool for their use
    D. convince all executives that they need to display confidence in the organization's rules

Questions 23-25.

DIRECTIONS: Questions 23 through 25 are to be answered on the basis of the following situation. Richard Ford, a top administrator, is responsible for output in his organization. Because productivity had been lagging for two periods in a row, Ford decided to establish a committee of his subordinate managers to investigate the reasons for the poor performance and to make recommendations for improvements. After two meetings, the committee came to the conclusions and made the recommendations that follow:

Output forecasts had been handed down from the top without prior consultation with middle management and first level supervision. Lines of authority and responsibility had been unclear. The planning and control process should be decentralized.
After receiving the committee's recommendations, Ford proceeded to take the following actions:
Ford decided he would retain final authority to establish quotas but would delegate to the middle managers the responsibility for meeting quotas.
After receiving Ford's decision, the middle managers proceeded to delegate to the first-line supervisors the authority to establish their own quotas. The middle managers eventually received and combined the first-line supervisors' quotas so that these conformed with Ford's.

23. Ford's decision to delegate responsibility for meeting quotas to the middle managers is INCONSISTENT with sound management principles because of which one of the following?
    A. Ford shouldn't have involved himself in the first place.
    B. Middle managers do not have the necessary skills.

C. Quotas should be established by the chief executive.
D. Responsibility should not be delegated.

24. The principle of co-extensiveness of responsibility and authority bears on Ford's decision.
In this case, it IMPLIES that
   A. authority should exceed responsibility
   B. authority should be delegated to match the degree of responsibility
   C. both authority and responsibility should be retained and not delegated
   D. responsibility should be delegated but authority should be retained

24.____

25. The middle manager's decision to delegate to the first-line supervisors the authority to establish quotas was INCORRECTLY reasoned because
   A. delegation and control must go together
   B. first-line supervisors are in no position to establish quotas
   C. one cannot delegate authority that one does not possess
   D. the meeting of quotas should not be delegated

25.____

KEY (CORRECT ANSWERS)

1.	A		11.	A
2.	C		12.	B
3.	A		13.	D
4.	C		14.	B
5.	C		15.	A
6.	B		16.	C
7.	D		17.	D
8.	B		18.	D
9.	B		19.	B
10.	C		20.	B

21. C
22. B
23. D
24. B
25. C

TEST 3

DIRECTIONS: Each question or incomplete statement is followed by several suggested answers or completions. Select the one that BEST answers the question or completes the statement. *PRINT THE LETTER OF THE CORRECT ANSWER IN THE SPACE AT THE RIGHT.*

1. A danger which exists in any organization as complex as that required for administration of a large public agency is that each department comes to believe that it exists for its own sake.
   The one of the following which has been attempted in some organizations as a cure for this condition is to
   A. build up the departmental esprit de corps
   B. expand the functions and jurisdictions of the various departments so that better integration is possible
   C. develop a body of specialists in the various subject matter fields which cut across departmental lines
   D. delegate authority to the lowest possible echelon
   E. systematically transfer administrative personnel from one department to another

1.____

2. At best, the organization chart is ordinarily and necessarily an idealized picture of the intent of top management, a reflection of hopes and aims rather than a photograph of the operating facts within the organization.
   The one of the following which is the basic reason for this is that the organization chart
   A. does not show the flow of work within the organization
   B. speaks in terms of positions rather than of live employees
   C. frequently contains unresolved internal ambiguities
   D. is a record of past organization or proposed future organization and never a photograph of the living organization
   E. does not label the jurisdiction assigned to each component unit

2.____

3. The drag of inadequacy is always downward. The need in administration is always for the reverse; for a department head to project his thinking to the city level, for the unit chief to try to see the problems of the department.
   The inability of a city administration to recruit administrators who can satisfy this need usually results in departments characterized by
   A. disorganization   B. poor supervision
   C. circumscribed viewpoints D. poor public relations
   E. a lack of programs

3.____

4. When, as a result of a shift in public sentiment, the elective officers of a city are changed, is it desirable for career administrators to shift ground without performing any illegal or dishonest act in order to conform to the policies of the new elective officers?
   A. *No*; the opinions and beliefs of the career officials are the result of long experience in administration and are more reliable than those of politicians

4.____

B. *Yes*; only in this way can citizens, political officials, and career administrators alike have confidence in the performance of their respective functions
C. *No*; a top career official who is so spineless as to change his views or procedures as a result of public opinion is of little value to the public service
D. *Yes*; legal or illegal, it is necessary that a city employee carry out the orders of his superior officers
E. *No*; shifting ground with every change in administration will preclude the use of a constant overall policy

5. Participation in developing plans which will affect levels in the organization in addition to his own, will contribute to an individual's understanding of the entire system. When possible, this should be encouraged.
This policy is, in general,
   A. *desirable*; the maintenance of any organization depends upon individual understanding
   B. *undesirable*; employees should participate only in these activities which affect their own level, otherwise conflicts in authority may arise
   C. *desirable*; an employee's will to contribute to the maintenance of an organization depends to a great extent on the level which he occupies
   D. *undesirable*; employees can be trained more efficiently and economically in an organized training program than by participating in plan development
   E. *desirable*; it will enable the employee to make intelligent suggestions for adjustment of the plan in the future

5.____

6. Constant study should be made of the information contained in reports to isolate those elements of experience which are static, those which are variable and repetitive, and those which are variable and due to chance.
Knowledge of those elements of experience in his organization which are static or constant will enable the operating official to
   A. fix responsibility for their supervisor at a lower level
   B. revise the procedure in order to make the elements variable
   C. arrange for follow-up and periodic adjustment
   D. bring related data together
   E. provide a frame of reference within which detailed standards for measurement can be installed

6.____

7. A chief staff officer, serving as one of the immediate advisors to the department head, has demonstrated a special capacity for achieving internal agreements and for sound judgment. As a result he has been used more and more as a source of counsel and assistance by the department head. Other staff officers and line officials as well have discovered that it is wise for them to check with this colleague in advance on all problematical matters handed up to the department head.

7.____

Developments such as this are
- A. *undesirable*; they disrupt the normal lines for flow of work in an organization
- B. *desirable*; they allow an organization to make the most of its strength wherever such strength resides
- C. *undesirable*; they tend to undermine the authority of the department head and put it in the hands of a staff officer who does not have the responsibility
- D. *desirable*; they tend to resolve internal ambiguities in organization
- E. *undesirable*; they make for bad morale by causing *cutthroat* competition

8. A common difference among executives is that some are not content unless they are out in front of everything that concerns their organization, while others prefer to run things by pulling strings, by putting others out in front and by stepping into the breach only when necessary.
Generally speaking, an advantage this latter method of operation has over the former is that it
    - A. results in a higher level of morale over a sustained period of time
    - B. gets results by exhortation and direct stimulus
    - C. makes it unnecessary to calculate integrated moves
    - D. makes the personality of the executive felt further down the line
    - E. results in the executive getting the reputation for being a good fellow

8.____

9. Administrators frequently have to get facts by interviewing people. Although the interview is a legitimate fact gathering technique, it has definite limitations which should not be overlooked.
The one of the following which is an important limitation is that
    - A. people who are interviewed frequently answer questions with guesses rather than admit their ignorance
    - B. it is a poor way to discover the general attitude and thinking of supervisors interviewed
    - C. people sometimes hesitate to give information during an interview which they will submit in written form
    - D. it is a poor way to discover how well employees understand departmental policies
    - E. the material obtained from the interview can usually be obtained at lower cost from existing records

9.____

10. It is desirable and advantageous to leave a maximum measure of planning responsibility to operating agencies or units, rather than to remove the responsibility to a central planning staff agency.
Adoption of the former policy (decentralized planning) would lead to
    - A. *less effective planning*; operating personnel do not have the time to make long-term plans
    - B. *more effective planning*; operating units are usually better equipped technically than any staff agency and consequently are in a better position to set up valid plans
    - C. *less effective planning*; a central planning agency has a more objective point of view than any operating agency can achieve

10.____

D. *more effective planning*; plans are conceived in terms of the existing situation and their execution is carried out with the will to succeed
E. *less effective planning*; there is little or no opportunity to check deviation from plans in the proposed set-up

Questions 11-15.

DIRECTIONS: The following sections appeared in a report on the work production of two bureaus of a department. Base your answers to Questions 11 through 15 on this information. Throughout the report, assume that each month has 4 weeks.

Each of the two bureaus maintains a chronological file. In Bureau A, every 9 months on the average, this material fills a standard legal size cabinet sufficient for 12,000 work units. In Bureau B the same type of cabinet is filled in 18 months. Each bureau maintains three complete years of information plus a current file. When the current file cabinet is filled, the cabinet containing the oldest material is emptied, the contents disposed of, and the cabinet used for current material. The similarity of these operations makes it possible to consolidate these files with little effort.

Study of the practice of using typists as filing clerks for periods when there is no typing work showed: (1) Bureau A has for the past 6 months completed a total of 1,500 filing work units a week using on the average 100 man-hours of trained file clerk time and 20 man-hours of typist time; (2) Bureau B has in the same period completed a total of 2,000 filing work units a week using on the average 125 man-hours of trained file clerk time and 60 hours of typist time. This includes all work in chronological files. Assuming that all clerks work at the same speed and that all typists work at the same speed, this indicates that work other than filing should be found for typists or that they should be given some training in the filing procedures used. It should be noted that Bureau A has not been producing the 1,600 units of technical (not filing) work per 30-day period required by Schedule K, but is at present 200 units behind. The Bureau should be allowed 3 working days to get on schedule.

11. What percentage (approximate) of the total number of filing work units completed in both units consists of the work involved in the maintenance of the chronological files?
   A. 5%   B. 10%   C. 15%   D. 20%   E. 25%

12. If the two chronological files are consolidated, the number of months which should be allowed for filling a cabinet is
   A. 2   B. 4   C. 6   D. 8   E. 14

13. The MAXIMUM number of file cabinets which can be released for other uses as a result of the consolidation recommended is
   A. 0
   B. 1
   C. 2
   D. 3
   E. not determinable on the basis of the data given

5 (#3)

14. If all the filing work for both units is consolidated without diminution in the amount to be done and all filing work is done by trained file clerks, the number of clerks required (35-hour work week) is   14.____
    A. 4   B. 5   C. 6   D. 7   E. 8

15. In order to comply with the recommendation with respect to Schedule K, the present work production of Bureau A must be increased by   15.____
    A. 50%
    B. 100%
    C. 150%
    D. 200%
    E. an amount which is not determinable

16. A certain training program during World War II resulted in the training of thousands of supervisors in industry. The methods of this program were later successfully applied in various government agencies. The program was based upon the assumption that there is an irreducible minimum of three supervisory skills.   16.____
    The one of these skills among the following is
    A. to know how to perform the job at hand well
    B. to be able to deal personally with workers, especially face-to-face
    C. to be able to imbue workers with the will to perform the job well
    D. to know the kind of work that is done by one's unit and the policies and procedures of one's agency
    E. the *know-how* of administrative and supervisory processes

17. A comment made by an employee about a training course was, "*We never have any idea how we ae getting along in that course.*"   17.____
    The fundamental error in training methods to which this criticism points is
    A. insufficient student participation
    B. failure to develop a feeling of need or active want for the material being presented
    C. the training sessions may be too long
    D. no attempt may have been made to connect the new material with what was already known
    E. no goals have been set for the students

18. Assume that you are attending a departmental conference on efficiency ratings at which it is proposed that a man-to-man rating scale be introduced.   18.____
    You should point out that, of the following, the CHIEF weakness of the man-to-man rating scale is that
    A. it involves abstract numbers rather than concrete employee characteristics
    B. judges are unable to select their own standards for comparison
    C. the standard for comparison shifts from man-to-man for each person rated
    D. not every person rated is given the opportunity to serve as a standard for comparison
    E. standards for comparison will vary from judge to judge

19. Assume that you are conferring with a supervisor who has assigned to his subordinates efficiency ratings which you believe to be generally too low. The supervisor argues that his ratings are generally low because his subordinates are generally inferior.
    Of the following, the evidence MOST relevant to the point at issue can be secured by comparing efficiency ratings assigned by the supervisor
    A. with ratings assigned by other supervisors in the same agency
    B. this year with ratings assigned by him in previous years
    C. to men recently transferred to his unit with ratings previously earned by these men
    D. with the general city average of ratings assigned by all supervisors to all employees
    E. with the relative order of merit of his employees as determined independently by promotion test marks

19.____

20. The one of the following which is NOT among the most common of the compensable factors used in wage evaluation studies is
    A. initiative and ingenuity required
    B. physical demand
    C. responsibility for the safety of others
    D. working conditions
    E. presence of avoidable hazards

20.____

21. If independent functions are separated, there is an immediate gain in conserving special skills. If we are to make optimum use of the abilities of our employees, these skills must be conserved.
    Assuming the correctness of this statement, it follows that
    A. if we are not making optimum use of employee abilities, independent functions have not been separated
    B. we are making optimum uses of employee abilities if we conserve special skills
    C. we are making optimum use of employee abilities if independent functions have been separated
    D. we are not making optimum use of employee abilities if we do not conserve special skills
    E. if special skills are being conserved, independent functions need not be separated

21.____

22. A reorganization of the bureau to provide for a stenographic pool instead of individual unit stenographers will result in more stenographic help being available to each unit when it is required, and consequently will result in greater productivity for each unit. An analysis of the space requirements shows that setting up a stenographic pool will require a minimum of 400 square feet of good space. In order to obtain this space, it will be necessary to reduce the space available for technical personnel, resulting in lesser productivity for each unit.

22.____

On the basis of the above discussion, it can be stated that, in order to obtain greater productivity for each unit,
- A. a stenographic pool should be set up
- B. further analysis of the space requirement should be made
- C. it is not certain as to whether or not a stenographic pool should be set up
- D. the space available for each technician should be increased in order to compensate for the absence of a stenographic pool
- E. a stenographic pool should not be set up

23. The adoption of single consolidated form will mean that most of the form will not be used in any one operation. This would create waste and confusion. This conclusion is based upon the unstated hypothesis that
    - A. if waste and confusion are to be avoided, a single consolidated form should be used
    - B. if a single consolidated form is constructed, most of it can be used in each operation
    - C. if waste and confusion are to be avoided, most of the form employed should be used
    - D. most of a single consolidation form is not used
    - E. a single consolidated form should not be used

23.____

KEY (CORRECT ANSWERS)

1.	E		11.	C
2.	B		12.	C
3.	C		13.	B
4.	B		14.	D
5.	E		15.	E
6.	A		16.	B
7.	B		17.	E
8.	A		18.	E
9.	A		19.	C
10.	D		20.	E

21. D
22. C
23. C

EXAMINATION SECTION
TEST 1

DIRECTIONS: Each question or incomplete statement is followed by several suggested answers or completions. Select the one that BEST answers the question or completes the statement. *PRINT THE LETTER OF THE CORRECT ANSWER IN THE SPACE AT THE RIGHT.*

1. A management approach widely used today is based on the belief that decisions should be made and actions should be taken by managers closest to the organization's problems.
   This style of management is MOST appropriately called _____ management.
   A. scientific
   B. means-end
   C. decentralized
   D. internal process

   1.____

2. As contrasted with tall organization structures with narrow spans of control, flat organization structures with wide spans of control MOST usually provide
   A. fast communication and information flows
   B. more levels in the organizational hierarchy
   C. fewer workers reporting to supervisors
   D. lower motivation because of tighter control standards

   2.____

3. Use of the systems approach is MOST likely to lead to
   A. consideration of the impact on the whole organization of actions taken in any part of that organization
   B. the placing of restrictions on departmental activity
   C. use of mathematical models to suboptimize production
   D. consideration of the activities of each unit of an organization as a totality without regard to the remainder of the organization

   3.____

4. An administrator, with overall responsibility for all administrative operations in a large operating agency, is considering organizing the agency's personnel office around either of the following two alternative concepts:
   Alternative I: A corps of specialists for each branch of personnel subject matter, whose skills, counsel, or work products are coordinated only by the agency personnel officer
   Alternative II: A crew of so-called *personnel generalists*, who individually work with particular segments of the organization but deal with all subspecialties of the personnel function
   The one of the following which MOST tends to be a DRAWBACK of Alternative I, as compared with Alternative II, is that
   A. training and employee relations work call for education, interests, and talents that differ from those required for classification and compensation work
   B. personnel office staff may develop only superficial familiarity with the specialized areas to which they have been assigned

   4.____

C. supervisors may fail to get continuing overall personnel advice on an integrated basis
D. the personnel specialists are likely to become so interested in and identified with the operating view as to particular cases that they lose their professional objectivity and become merely advocates of what some supervisor wants

5. The matrix summary or decision matrix is a useful tool for making choices. Its effectiveness is MOST dependent upon the user's ability to
   A. write a computer program (Fortran or Cobol)
   B. assign weights representing the relative importance of the objectives
   C. solve a set of two equations with two unknowns
   D. work with matrix algebra

6. An organizational form which is set up only on an *ad hoc* basis to meet specific goals is said PRIMARILY to use
   A. clean break departmentation
   B. matrix or task force organization
   C. scalar specialization
   D. geographic or area-wide decentralization

7. The concept of job enlargement would LEAST properly be implemented by
   A. permitting workers to follow through on tasks or projects from start to finish
   B. delegating the maximum authority possible for decision-making to lower levels in the hierarchy
   C. maximizing the number of professional classes in the classification plan
   D. training employees to grow beyond whatever tasks they have been performing

8. As used in the area of admission, the principle of *unity of command* MOST specifically means that
   A. an individual should report to only one superior for any single activity
   B. individuals make better decisions than do committees
   C. in large organizations, chains of command are normally too long
   D. an individual should not supervise over five subordinates

9. The method of operations research, statistical decision-making, and linear programming have been referred to as the tool kit of the manager. Utilization of these tools is LEAST useful in the performance of which of the following functions?
   A. Elimination of the need for using judgment when making decisions
   B. Facilitation of decision-making without the need for sub-optimization
   C. Quantifying problems for management study
   D. Research and analysis of management operations

10. When acting in their respective managerial capacities, the chief executive officer and the office supervisor both perform the fundamental functions of management.
    Of the following differences between the two, the one which is generally considered to be the LEAST significant is the
    A. breadth of the objectives
    B. complexity of measuring actual efficiency of performance
    C. number of decisions made
    D. organizational relationships affected by actions taken

11. The ability of operations researchers to solve complicated problems rests on their use of models.
    These models can BEST be described as
    A. mathematical statements of the problem
    B. physical constructs that simulate a work layout
    C. toy-like representations of employees in work environments
    D. role-playing simulations

12. Of the following, it is MOST likely to be proper for the agency head to allow the agency personnel officer to make final selection of appointees from certified eligible lists where there are
    A. *small* numbers of employees to be hired in newly-developed professional fields
    B. *large* numbers of persons to be hired for key managerial positions
    C. *large* numbers of persons to be hired in very routine occupations where the individual discretion of operating officials is not vital
    D. *small* numbers of persons to be hired in highly specialized professional occupations which are vital to the agency's operations

13. Of the following, an operating agency personnel office is LEAST likely to be able to exert strong influence or control within the operating agency by
    A. interpreting to the operating agency head what is intended by the directives and rules emanating from the central personnel agency
    B. establishing the key objectives of those line divisions of the operating agency employing large numbers of staff and operating under the management-by-objectives approach
    C. formulating and proposing to the agency head the internal policies and procedures on personnel matters required within the operating agency
    D. exercising certain discretionary authority in the application of the agency head's general personnel policies to actual specific situations

14. PERT is a recently developed system used PRIMARILY to
    A. evaluate the quality of applicants' background
    B. analyze and control the timing aspects of a major project
    C. control the total expenditure of agency funds within a monthly or quarterly time period
    D. analyze and control the differential effect on costs of purchasing different quantities

15. Assume that an operating agency has among its vacant positions two positions, each of which encompasses mixed duties. Both require appointees to have considerable education and experience, but these requirements are essential only for the more difficult duties of these positions. In the place of these positions, an administrator creates two new positions, one in which the higher duties are concentrated and the other with the lesser functions requiring only minimum preparation.
Of the following, it is generally MOST appropriate to characterize the administrator's action as a(n)
    A. *undesirable* example of deliberate downgrading of standards and requirements
    B. *undesirable* manipulation of the classification system for non-merit purposes
    C. *desirable* broadening of the definition of a class of positions
    D. *desirable* example of job redesign

16. Of the following, the LEAST important stumbling block to the development of personnel mobility among governmental jurisdictions is the
    A. limitations on lateral entry above junior levels in many jurisdictions
    B. continued collection of filing fees for civil service tests by many governmental jurisdictions
    C. absence of reciprocal exchange of retirement benefit eligibility between governments
    D. disparities in salary scales between governments

17. Of the following, the MAJOR disadvantage of a personnel system that features the *selection out* (forced retirement) of those who have been passed over a number of times for promotion is that such a system
    A. wastes manpower which is perfectly competent at one level but unable to rise above that level
    B. wastes funds by requiring review boards
    C. leads to excessive recruiting of newcomers from outside the system
    D. may not be utilized in *closed* career systems with low maximum age limits for entrance

18. Of the following, the fields in which operating agency personnel offices generally exercise the MOST stringent controls over first line supervisors in the agency are
    A. methods analysis and work simplification
    B. selection and position classification
    C. vestibule training and Gantt chart
    D. suggestion systems and staff development

19. Of the following, computers are normally MOST effective in handling
    A. large masses of data requiring simple processing
    B. small amounts of data requiring constantly changing complex processing
    C. data for which reported values are often subject to inaccuracies
    D. large amounts of data requiring continual programming and reprocessing

20. Contingency planning, which has long been used by the military and is assuming increasing importance in other organizations, may BEST be described as a process which utilizes
    A. alternative plans based on varying assumptions
    B. *crash programs* by organizations departmentalized along process lines
    C. plans which mandate substitution of equipment for manpower at predetermined operational levels
    D. plans that individually and accurately predict future events

21. In the management of inventory, two kinds of costs normally determine when to order and in what amounts.
    The one of the following choices which includes BOTH of these kinds of costs is _____ costs and _____ costs.
    A. carrying; storage
    B. personnel; order
    C. computer; order
    D. personnel; computer

22. At top management levels, the one of the following which is generally the MOST important executive skill is skill in
    A. budgeting procedures
    B. a technical discipline
    C. controlling actions in accordance with previously approved plans
    D. seeing the organization as a whole

23. Of the following, the BEST way to facilitate the successful operation of a committee is to set guidelines establishing its
    A. budget exclusive of personnel costs
    B. location
    C. schedule of meetings or conferences
    D. scope of purpose

24. Executive training programs that single out particular managers and groom them for promotion create the so-called organizational *crown princes*.
    Of the following, the MOST serious problem that arises in connection with this practice is that
    A. the managers chosen for promotion seldom turn out to be the best managers since the future potential of persons cannot be predicted
    B. not enough effort is made to remove organizational obstacles in the way of their development and achievement
    C. the resentment of the managers not selected for the program has an adverse effect on the motivation of those managers not selected
    D. performance appraisal and review are not carried out systematically enough

25. Of the following, the LEAST likely result of the use of the concept of job enlargement is that
    A. coordination will be simplified
    B. the individual's job will become less challenging
    C. worker satisfaction will increase
    D. fewer people will have to give attention to each piece of work

KEY (CORRECT ANSWERS)

1. C
2. A
3. A
4. C
5. B
6. B
7. C
8. A
9. A
10. C
11. A
12. C
13. B
14. B
15. D
16. B
17. A
18. B
19. A
20. A
21. A
22. D
23. D
24. C
25. B

TEST 2

DIRECTIONS: Each question or incomplete statement is followed by several suggested answers or completions. Select the one that BEST answers the question or completes the statement. *PRINT THE LETTER OF THE CORRECT ANSWER IN THE SPACE AT THE RIGHT.*

1. The one of the following which is MOST likely to be emphasized in the use of the brainstorming technique is the
    A. early consideration of cost factors of all ideas which may be suggested
    B. avoidance of impractical suggestions
    C. separation of the generation of ideas from their evaluation
    D. appraisal of suggestions concurrently with their initial presentation

   1.____

2. Of the following, the BEST method for assessing managerial performance is generally to
    A. compare the manager's accomplishments against clear, specific, agreed-upon goals
    B. compare the manager's traits with those of his peers on a predetermined objective
    C. measure the manager's behavior against a listing of itemized personal traits
    D. measure the manager's success according to the enumeration of the *satisfaction* principle

   2.____

3. As compared with recruitment from outside, selection from within the service must generally show GREATER concern for the
    A. prestige in which the public service as a whole is held by the public
    B. morale of the candidate group compromising the recruitment field
    C. cost of examining per candidate
    D. benefits of the use of standardized and validated tests

   3.____

4. Performance budgeting focuses PRIMARY attention upon which one of the following? The
    A. things to be acquired, such as supplies and equipment
    B. general character and relative importance of the work to be done or the service to be rendered
    C. list of personnel to be employed, by specific title
    D. separation of employee performance evaluations from employee compensation

   4.____

5. Of the following, the FIRST step in the installation and operation of a performance budgeting system generally should be the
    A. identification of program costs in relationship to the accounting system and operating structure
    B. identification of the specific end results of past programs in other jurisdictions

   5.____

C. identification of work programs that are meaningful for management purposes
D. establishment of organizational structures each containing only one work program

6. Of the following, the MOST important purpose of a system of quarterly allotments of appropriated funds generally is to enable the
   A. head of the judicial branch to determine the legality of agency requests for budget increases
   B. operating agencies of government to upgrade the quality of their services without increasing costs
   C. head of the executive branch to control the rate at which the operating agencies obligate and expend funds
   D. operating agencies of government to avoid payment for services which have not been properly rendered by employees

7. In the preparation of the agency's budget, the agency's central budget office has two responsibilities: program review and management improvement. Which one of the following questions concerning an operating agency's program is MOST closely related to the agency budget officer's program review responsibility?
   A. Can expenditures for supplies, materials, or equipment be reduced?
   B. Will improved work methods contribute to a more effective program?
   C. What is the relative importance of this program as compared to a higher level of program performance?
   D. Will a realignment of responsibilities contribute to a higher level of program performance?

8. Of the following, the method of evaluating relative rates of return normally and generally thought to be MOST useful in evaluating government operations is _____ analysis.
   A. cost-benefit
   B. budget variance
   C. investment capital
   D. budget planning program

9. The one of the following assumptions that is LEAST likely to be made by a democratic or permissive type of leader is that
   A. commitment to goals is seldom a result of monetary rewards alone
   B. people can learn not only to accept, but also to seek, responsibility
   C. the average person prefers security over advancement
   D. creativity may be found in most segments of the population

10. In attempting to motivate subordinates, a manager should PRINCIPALLY be aware of the fact that
    A. the psychological qualities of people, in general, are easily predictable
    B. fear, as a traditional form of motivation, has lost much of its former power to motivate people in our modern industrial society
    C. fear is still the most potent force in motivating the behavior of subordinates in the public service
    D. the worker has very little control over the quality and quantity of his output

11. Assume that the following figures represent the number of work-unit that were produced during a week by each of sixteen employees in a division:

        12   16   13   18
        21   12   16   13
        16   13   17   21
        13   15   18   20

If all of the employees of the division who produced thirteen work-units during the week had instead produced fifteen work-units during that same week, then for that week the
   A. mean, median, and mode would all change
   B. mean and mode would change, but the median would remain the same
   C. mode and median would change, but the mean would remain the same
   D. mode, mean, and median would all still remain unchanged in value

12. An important law in motivation theory is called the *law of effect*. This law says that behavior which satisfies a person's needs tends to be repeated; behavior which does not satisfy a person's needs tends to be eliminated.
The one of the following which is the BEST interpretation of this law is that
   A. productivity depends on personality traits
   B. diversity of goals leads to instability and motivation
   C. the greater the satisfaction, the more likely it is that the behavior will be reinforced
   D. extrinsic satisfaction is more important than intrinsic reward

13. Of the following, the MOST acceptable reason an administrator can give for taking advice from other employees in the organization only when he asks for it is that he wants to
   A. encourage creativity and high morale
   B. keep dysfunctional pressures and inconsistent recommendations to a minimum
   C. show his superiors and peers who is in charge
   D. show his subordinates who is in charge

14. A complete picture of the communication channels in an organization can BEST be revealed by
   A. observing the planned paperwork system
   B. recording the highly intermittent patterns of communication
   C. plotting the entire flow of information over a period of time
   D. monitoring the *grapevine*

Questions 15-16.

DIRECTIONS: Questions 15 and 16 are to be answered SOLELY on the basis of the following passage.

Management by objectives (MBO) may be defined as the process by which the superior and the subordinate managers of an organization jointly define its common goals, define each individual's major areas of responsibility in terms of the results expected of him and use these measures as guides for operating the unit and assessing the contribution of each of its members.

The MBO approach requires that after organizational goals are established and communicated, targets must be set for each individual position which are congruent with organizational goals. Periodic performance reviews and a final review using the objectives set as criteria are also basic to this approach.

Recent studies have shown that MBO programs are influenced by attitudes and perceptions of the boss, the company, the reward-punishment system, and the program itself. In addition, the manner in which the MBO program is carried out can influence the success of the program. A study done in the late sixties indicates that the best results are obtained when the manager sets goals which deal with significant problem areas in the organizational unit, or with the subordinate's personal deficiencies. These goals must be clear with regard to what is expected of the subordinate. The frequency of feedback is also important in the success of a management-by-objectives program. Generally, the greater the amount of feedback, the more successful the MBO program.

15. According to the above passage, the expected output for individual employees should be determined 15.____
    A. after a number of reviews of work performance
    B. after common organizational goals are defined
    C. before common organizational goals are defined
    D. on the basis of an employee's personal qualities

16. According to the above passage, the management-by-objectives approach requires 16.____
    A. less feedback than other types of management programs
    B. little review of on-the-job performance after the initial setting of goals
    C. general conformance between individual goals and organizational goals
    D. the setting of goals which deal with minor problem area in the organization

Questions 17-19.

DIRECTIONS: Questions 17 through 19 are to be answered SOLELY on the basis of the following passage.

During the last decade, a great deal of interest has been generated around the phenomenon of organizational development, or the process of developing human resources through conscious organization effort. Organizational development (OD) stresses improving interpersonal relationships and organizational skills, such as communication, to a much greater degree than individual training ever did.

The kind of training that an organization should emphasize depends upon the present and future structure of the organization. If future organizations are to be unstable, shifting coalitions, then individual skills and abilities, particularly those emphasizing innovativeness, creativity, flexibility, and the latest technological knowledge, are crucial, and individual training is most appropriate.

But if there is to be little change in organizational structure, then the main thrust of training should be group-oriented or organizational development. This approach seems better designed for overcoming hierarchical barriers, for developing a degree of interpersonal relationships which make communication along the chain of command possible, and for retaining a modicum of innovation and/or flexibility.

17. According to the above passage, group-oriented training is MOST useful in
    A. developing a communications system that will facilitate understanding through the chain of command
    B. highly flexible and mobile organizations
    C. preventing the crossing of hierarchical barriers within an organization
    D. saving energy otherwise wasted on developing methods of dealing with rigid hierarchies

17.____

18. The one of the following conclusions which can be drawn MOST appropriately from the above passage is that
    A. behavioral research supports the use of organizational development training method rather than individualized training
    B. it is easier to provide individualized training in specific skills than to set up sensitivity training programs
    C. organizational development eliminates innovative or flexible activity
    D. the nature of an organization greatly influences which training methods will be most effective

18.____

19. According to the above passage, the one of the following which is LEAST important for large-scale organizations geared to rapid and abrupt change is
    A. current technological information
    B. development of a high degree of interpersonal relationships
    C. development of individual skills and abilities
    D. emphasis on creativity

19.____

Questions 20-25.

DIRECTIONS: Each of Questions 20 through 25 consist of a statement which contains one word that is incorrectly used because it is not in keeping with the meaning that the quotation is evidently intended to convey. Determine which word is INCORRECTLY used. Select from the choices lettered A, B, C, and D the word which, when substituted for the incorrectly used word, would BEST help to convey the meaning of the statement.

20. One of the considerations likely to affect the currency of classification, particularly in professional and managerial occupations, is the impact of the incumbent's capacities on the job. Some work is highly susceptible to change as the result of the special talents or interests of the classifier. Organization should never be so rigid as not to capitalize on the innovative or unusual proclivities of its key employees. While a machine operator may not be able, even subtly, to change the character or level of his job, the design engineer, the attorney, or the organization and methods analyst might readily do so. Reliance on his judgment and the scope of his assignments may both grow as the result of his skill, insight, and capacity.
    A. unlikely   B. incumbent   C. directly   D. scope

21. The supply of services by the state is not governed by market price. The aim is to supply such services to all who need them and to treat all consumers equally. This objective especially compels the civil servant to maintain a role f strict impartiality, based on the principle of equality of individual citizens vis-à-vis their government. However, there is a clear difference between being neutral and impartial. If the requirement is construed to mean that all civil servants should be political eunuchs, devoid of the drive and motivation essential to dynamic administration, then the concept of impartiality is being seriously utilized. Modern governments should not be stopped from demanding that their hirelings have not only the technical but the emotional qualifications necessary for whole-hearted effort.
    A. determined   B. rule   C. stable   D. misapplied

22. The manager was barely listening. Recently, at the divisional level, several new fronts of troubles had erupted, including a requirement to increase production yet hold down operating costs and somehow raise quality standards. Though the three objectives were basically obsolete, top departmental management was insisting on the simultaneous attainment of them, an insistence not helping the manager's ulcer, an old enemy within. Thus, the manager could not find time for interest in individuals—only in statistics which regiment of individuals, like unconsidered Army privates, added up to.
    A. quantity   B. battalion   C. incompatible   D. quiet

23. When a large volume of data flows directly between operators and first-line supervisors, senior executives tend to be out of the mainstream of work. Summary reports can increase their remoteness. An executive needs to know the volume, quality, and cost of completed work, and exceptional problems. In addition, he may desire information on key operating conditions. Summary reports on these matters are, therefore, essential features of a communications network and make delegation without loss of control possible.
    A. unimportant   B. quantity   C. offset   D. incomplete

24. Of major significance in management is harmony between the overall objectives of the organization and the managerial objectives within that organization. In addition, harmony among goals of managers is impossible; they should not be at cross-purposes. Each manager's goal should supplement and assist the goals of his colleagues. Likewise, the objectives of individuals or non-management members should be harmonized with those of the manager. When this is accomplished, genuine teamwork is the result, and human relations are aided materially. The integration of managers' and individuals' goals aids in achieving greater work satisfaction at all levels.
    A. competition   B. dominate   C. incremental   D. vital

24.____

25. Change constantly challenges the manager. Some of this change is evolutionary, some revolutionary, some recognizable, some non-recognizable. Both forces within an enterprise and forces outside the enterprise cause managers to act and react in initiating changes in their immediate working environment. Change invalidates existing operations. Goals are not being accomplished in the best manner, problems develop, and frequently because of the lack of time, only patched-up solutions are followed. The result is that the mode of management is profound in nature and temporary in effectiveness. A complete overhaul of managerial operations should take place. It appears quite likely that we are just beginning to see the real effects of change in our society; the pace probably will accelerate in ways that few really understand or know how to handle.
    A. confirms   B. decline   C. instituting   D. superficial

25.____

KEY (CORRECT ANSWERS)

1.	C	11.	B
2.	A	12.	C
3.	B	13.	B
4.	B	14.	C
5.	C	15.	B
6.	C	16.	C
7.	C	17.	A
8.	A	18.	D
9.	C	19.	B
10.	B	20.	B

21. D
22. C
23. C
24. D
25. D

EXAMINATION SECTION
TEST 1

DIRECTIONS: Each question or incomplete statement is followed by several suggested answers or completions. Select the one that BEST answers the question or completes the statement. *PRINT THE LETTER OF THE CORRECT ANSWER IN THE SPACE AT THE RIGHT.*

1. An executive assigns A, the head of a staff unit, to devise plans for reducing the delay in submittal of reports by a local agency headed by C. The reports are under the supervision of C's subordinate line official B with whom A is to deal directly. In his investigation, A finds: (1) the reasons for the delay; and (2) poor practices which have either been overlooked or condoned by line official B.
   Of the following courses of action A could take, the BEST one would be to
   A. develop recommendations with line official B with regard to reducing the delay and correcting the poor practice and then report fully to his own executive
   B. discuss the findings with C in an attempt to correct the situation before making any formal report on the poor practices
   C. report both findings to his executive, attaching the explanation offered by C
   D. report to his executive on the first finding and discuss the second in a friendly way with line official B
   E. report the first finding to his executive, ignoring the second until his opinion is requested

   1.____

2. Drafts of a proposed policy, prepared by a staff committee, are circulated to ten member of the field staff of the organization by route slips with a request for comments within two weeks. Two members of the field staff make extensive comments, four offer editorial suggestions, and the remainder make minor favorable comments. Shortly after, it found that the statement needs considerable revision by the field staff.
   Of the following possible reasons for the original failure of the field staff to identify difficulties, the MOST likely is that the
   A. field staff did not take sufficient time to review the manual
   B. field staff had not been advised of the type of contribution expected
   C. low morale of the field staff prevented their showing interest
   D. policy statement was too advanced for the staff
   E. staff committee was not sufficiently representative

   2.____

3. Operator participation in management improvement work is LEAST likely to
   A. assure the use of best available management technique
   B. overcome the stigma of the outside expert
   C. place responsibility for improvement in the person who knows the job best
   D. simplify installation
   E. take advantage of the desire of most operators to seek self-improvement

   3.____

4. In general, the morale of workers in an agency is MOST frequently and MOST significantly affected by the
   A. agency policies of organizational structure and operational procedures
   B. distance of the employee's job from his home community
   C. fringe benefits
   D. number of opportunities for advancement
   E. relationship with supervisors

5. Of the following, the PRIMARY function of a work distribution chart is to
   A. analyze the soundness of existing divisions of labor
   B. eliminate the unnecessary clerical detail
   C. establish better supervisory techniques
   D. simplify work methods
   E. weed out core functions

6. In analyzing a process chart, which one of the following should be asked FIRST?
   A. How   B. When   C. Where   D. Who   E. Why

7. Which one of the following is NOT an advantage of the interview method of collecting data? It
   A. enables interviewer to judge the person interviewed on such matters as general attitude, knowledge, etc.
   B. helps build up personal relations for later installation of changes
   C. is a flexible method that can be adjusted to changing circumstances
   D. permits the obtaining of *off the record* information
   E. produces more accurate information than other methods

8. Which one of the following may be defined as a *regularly recurring appraisal of the manner in which all elements of agency management are being carried out*?
   A. Functional survey
   B. Operations audit
   C. Organization survey
   D. Over-all survey
   E. Reconnaissance survey

9. An analysis of the flow of work in a department should begin with the _____ work.
   A. major routine   B. minor routine   C. supervisory
   D. technical   E. unusual

10. Which method would MOST likely be used to get first-hand information on complaints from the public?
    A. Study of correspondence
    B. Study of work volume
    C. Tracing specific transactions through a series of steps
    D. Tracing use of forms
    E. Worker desk audit

11. People will generally produce the MOST if
    A. management exercises close supervision over the work
    B. there is strict discipline in the group
    C. they are happy in their work
    D. they feel involved in their work
    E. they follow *the one best way*

12. The normal analysis of which chart listed below is MOST closely related to organizational analysis? _____ chart.
    A. Layout   B. Operation   C. Process
    D. Work count   E. Work distribution

13. The work count would be LEAST helpful in accomplishing which one of the following?
    A. Demonstrating personnel needs   B. Improving the sequence of steps
    C. Measuring the value of a step   D. Spotting bottlenecks
    E. Stimulating interest in work

14. Which one of the following seems LEAST useful as a guide in interviewing an employee in a procedure and methods survey?
    A. Explaining who you are and the purpose of your visit
    B. Having a general plan of what you intend to get from the interview
    C. Listening carefully and not interrupting
    D. Trying out his reactions to your ideas for improvements
    E. Trying to analyze his reasons for saying what he says

15. Which one of the following is an advantage of the questionnaire method of gathering facts as compared with the interview method?
    A. Different people may interpret the questions differently
    B. Less *off the record* information is given
    C. More time may be taken in order to give exact answers
    D. Personal relationships with the people involved are not established
    E. There is less need for follow-up

16. Which one of the following is generally NOT an advantage of the personal observation method of gathering facts? It
    A. enables staff to use *off the record* information if personally observed
    B. helps in developing valid recommendations
    C. helps the person making the observation acquire *know how* valuable for later installation and follow-up
    D. is economical in time and money
    E. may turn up other problems in need of solution

17. Which of the following would MOST often be the best way to minimize resistance to change?
    A. Break the news about the change gently to the people affected
    B. Increase the salary of the people affected by the change
    C. Let the people concerned participate at the decision to change

D. Notify all people concerned with the change, both orally and in writing
E. Stress the advantages of the new system

18. The functional organization chart 18.____
    A. does not require periodic revision
    B. includes a description of the duties of each organization segment
    C. includes positions and titles for each organization segment
    D. is the simplest type of organization chart
    E. is used primarily by newly established agencies

19. The principle of span of control has frequently been said to be in conflict with the 19.____
    A. principle of unity of command
    B. principle that authority should be commensurate with responsibility
    C. principle that like functions should be grouped into one unit
    D. principle that the number of levels between the top of an organization and the bottom should be small
    E. scalar principle

20. If an executive delegates to his subordinates authority to handle problems of a routine nature for which standard solutions have been established, he may expect that 20.____
    A. fewer complaint will be received
    B. he has made it more difficult for his subordinates to solve these problems
    C. he has opened the way for confusion in his organization
    D. there will be a lack of consistency in the methods applied to the solution of these problems
    E. these routine problems will be handled efficiently and he will have more time for other non-routine work

21. Which of the following would MOST likely be achieved by a change in the basic organization structure from the *process* or *functional* type to the *purpose* or *product* type? 21.____
    A. Easier recruitment of personnel in a tight labor market
    B. Fixing responsibility at a lower level in the organization
    C. Greater centralization
    D. Greater economy
    E. Greater professional development

22. Usually the MOST difficult problem in connection with a major reorganization is 22.____
    A. adopting a pay plan to fit the new structure
    B. bringing the organization manual up-to-date
    C. determining the new organization structure
    D. gaining acceptance of the new plan by the higher level employees
    E. gaining acceptance of the new plan by the lower level employees

23. Which of the following statements MOST accurately describes the work of the chiefs of MOST staff divisions in departments?
Chiefs
    A. focus more on getting the job done than on how it is done
    B. are mostly interested in short-range results
    C. nearly always advise but rarely advise
    D. usually command or control but rarely advise
    E. provide service to the rest of the organization and/or assist the chief executive in planning and controlling operations

24. In determining the type of organization structure of an enterprise, the one factor that might be given relatively greater weight in a small organization than in a larger organization of the same nature is the
    A. geographical location of the enterprise
    B. individual capabilities of incumbents
    C. method of financing to be employed
    D. size of the area served
    E. type of activity engaged in

25. Functional foremanship differs MOST markedly from generally accepted principle of administration in that it advocates
    A. an unlimited span of control
    B. less delegation of responsibility
    C. more than one supervisor for an employee
    D. nonfunctional organization
    E. substitution of execution for planning

KEY (CORRECT ANSWERS)

1. A
2. B
3. A
4. E
5. A
6. E
7. E
8. B
9. A
10. A
11. D
12. E
13. B
14. D
15. C
16. D
17. C
18. B
19. D
20. E
21. B
22. D
23. E
24. B
25. C

TEST 2

DIRECTIONS: Each question or incomplete statement is followed by several suggested answers or completions. Select the one that BEST answers the question or completes the statement. *PRINT THE LETTER OF THE CORRECT ANSWER IN THE SPACE AT THE RIGHT.*

1. Decentralization of the authority to make decisions is a necessary result of increased complexity in an organization, but for the sake of efficiency and coordination of operations, such decentralization must be planned carefully. A good general rule is that
   A. any decision should be made at the lowest possible point in the organization where all the information and competence necessary for a sound decision are available
   B. any decision should be made at the highest possible point in the organization, thus guaranteeing the best decision
   C. any decision should be made at the lowest possible point in the organization, but always approved by management
   D. any decision should be made by management and referred to the proper subordinate for comment
   E. no decision should be made by any individual in the organization without approval by a superior

   1.____

2. One drawback of converting a conventional consecutive filing system to a terminal digit filing system for a large installation is that
   A. conversion would be expensive in time and manpower
   B. conversion would prevent the proper use of recognized numeric classification systems, such as the Dewey decimal, in classifying files material
   C. responsibility for proper filing cannot be pinpointed in the terminal digit system
   D. the terminal digit system requires considerably more space than a normal filing system

   2.____

3. The basic filing system that would ordinarily be employed in a large administrative headquarters unit is the _____ file system.
   A alphabetic   B. chronological
   C. mnemonic   D. retention
   E. subject classification

   3.____

4. A records center is of benefit in a records management program PRIMARILY because
   A. all the records of the organization are kept in one place
   B. inactive records can be stored economically in less expense storage areas
   C. it provides a place where useless records can be housed at little or no cost to the organization

   4.____

D. obsolete filing and storage equipment can be utilized out of view of the public
E. records analysts can examine an organization's files without affecting the unit's operation or upsetting the supervisors

5. In examining a number of different forms to see whether any could be combined or eliminated, which of the following would one be MOST likely to use?
   A. Forms analysis sheet of recurring data
   B. Forms control log
   C. Forms design and approval request
   D. Forms design and guide sheet
   E. Numerical file

6. The MOST important reason for control of *bootleg* forms is that
   A. they are more expensive than authorized forms
   B. they are usually poorly designed
   C. they can lead to unnecessary procedures
   D. they cannot be reordered as easily as authorized terms
   E. violation of rules and regulations should not be allowed

7. With a box design of a form, the caption title or question to be answered should be located in the _____ of the box.
   A. center at the bottom
   B. center at the top
   C. lower left corner
   D. lower right corner
   E. upper left corner

8. A two-part snapout form would be MOST properly justified if
   A. it is a cleaner operation
   B. it is prepared ten times a week
   C. it saves time in preparation
   D. it is to be filled out by hand rather than by typewriter
   E. proper registration is critical

9. When deciding whether or not to approve a request for a new form, which reference is normally MOST pertinent?
   A. Alphabetical Forms File
   B. Functional Forms File
   C. Numerical Forms File
   D. Project Completion Report
   E. Records Retention Data

10. Which of the following statements BEST explains the significance of the famed Hawthorne Plant experiments?
    They showed that
    A. a large span of control leads to more production than a small span of control
    B. morale has no relationship to production
    C. personnel counseling is of relatively little importance in a going organization

D. the special attention received by a group in an experimental situation has a greater impact on production than changes in working conditions
E. there is a direct relationship between the amount of illumination and production

11. Which of the following would most often NOT result from a highly efficient management control system?
    A. Facilitation of delegation
    B. Highlighting of problem areas
    C. Increase in willingness of people to experiment or to take calculated risks
    D. Provision of an objective test of new ideas or new methods and procedures
    E. Provision of information useful for revising objectives, programs, and operations

12. The PERT system is a
    A. method for laying out office space on a modular basis utilizing prefabricated partitions
    B. method of motivating personnel to be continuously alert and to improve their appearance
    C. method of program planning and control using a network or flow plan
    D. plan for expanding reporting techniques
    E. simplified method of cost accounting

13. The term *management control* is MOST frequently used to mean
    A. an objective and unemotional approach by management
    B. coordinating the efforts of all parts of the organization
    C. evaluation of results in relation to plan
    D. giving clear, precise orders to subordinates
    E. keeping unions from making managerial decisions

14. Which one of the following factors has the MOST bearing on the frequency with which a control report should be made?
    A. Degree of specialization of the work
    B. Degree of variability in activities
    C. Expense of the report
    D. Number of levels of supervision
    E. Number of personnel involved

15. The value of statistical records is MAINLY dependent upon the
    A. method of presenting the material
    B. number of items used
    C. range of cases sampled
    D. reliability of the information used
    E. time devoted to compiling the material

16. When a supervisor delegates an assignment, he should
    A. delegate his responsibility for the assignment
    B. make certain that the assignment is properly performed
    C. participate in the beginning and final stages of the assignment
    D. retail all authority needed to complete the assignment
    E. oversee all stages of the assignment

17. Assume that the department in which you are employed has never given official sanction to a mid-afternoon coffee break. Some bureaus have it and others do not. In the latter case, some individuals merely absent themselves for about 15 minutes at 3 P.M. while others remain on the job despite the fatigue which seems to be common among all employees in this department at that time.
    The course of action which you should recommend, if possible, is to
    A. arrange a schedule of mid-afternoon coffee breaks for all employees
    B. forbid all employees to take a mid-afternoon coffee break
    C. permit each bureau to decide for itself whether or not it will have a coffee break
    D. require all employees who wish a coffee break to take a shorter lunch period
    E. arrange a poll to discover the consensus of the department

18. The one of the following which is LEAST important in the management of a suggestion program is
    A. giving awards which are of sufficient value to encourage competition
    B. securing full support from the department's officers and executives
    C. publicizing the program and the awards given
    D. holding special conferences to analyze and evaluate some of the suggestions needed
    E. providing suggestion boxes in numerous locations

19. The one of the following which is MOST likely to decrease morale is
    A. insistence on strict adherence to safety rules
    B. making each employee responsible for the tidiness of his work area
    C. overlooking evidence of hostility between groups of employees
    D. strong, aggressive leadership
    E. allocating work on the basis of personal knowledge of the abilities and interests of the member of the department

20. Assume that a certain office procedure has been standard practice for many years.
    When a new employee asks why this particular procedure is followed, the supervisor should FIRST
    A. explain that everyone does it that way
    B. explain the reason for the procedure
    C. inform him that it has always been done that way in that particular office
    D. tell him to try it for a while before asking questions
    E. tell him he has never thought about it that way

21. Several employees complain informally to their supervisor regarding some new procedures which have been instituted.
    The supervisor should IMMEDIATELY
    A. explain that management is responsible
    B. state frankly that he had nothing to do with it
    C. refer the matter to the methods analyst
    D. tell the employees to submit their complaint as a formal grievance
    E. investigate the complaint

22. A new employee asks his supervisor how he is doing. Actually, he is not doing well in some phases of the job, but it is felt that he will learn in time.
    The BEST response for the supervisor to make is:
    A. Some things you are doing well, and in others I am sure you will improve.
    B. Wait until the end of your probation period when we will discuss this matter.
    C. You are not doing too well.
    D. You are doing very well.
    E. I'll be able to tell you when I go over your record.

23. The PRINCIPAL aim of a supervisor is to
    A. act as liaison between employee and management
    B. get the work done
    C. keep up morale
    D. train his subordinates
    E. become chief of the department

24. When the work of two bureaus must be coordinated, direct contact between the subordinates in each bureau who are working on the problem is
    A. *bad*, because it violates the chain of command
    B. *bad*, because they do not have authority to make decisions
    C. *good*, because it enable quicker results
    D. *good*, because it relieves their superiors of any responsibilities
    E. *bad*, because they may work at cross purposes

25. Of the following, the organization defect which can be ascertained MOST readily merely by analyzing an accurate and well-drawn organization chart is
    A. ineffectiveness of an activity
    B. improper span of control
    C. inappropriate assignment of functions
    D. poor supervision
    E. unlawful delegation of authority

KEY (CORRECT ANSWERS)

1. A
2. A
3. E
4. B
5. A

6. C
7. E
8. E
9. B
10. D

11. C
12. C
13. C
14. B
15. D

16. B
17. A
18. E
19. C
20. B

21. E
22. A
23. B
24. C
25. B

EXAMINATION SECTION
TEST 1

DIRECTIONS: Each question or incomplete statement is followed by several suggested answers or completions. Select the one that BEST answers the question or completes the statement. *PRINT THE LETTER OF THE CORRECT ANSWER IN THE SPACE AT THE RIGHT.*

1. The conventional wisdom about group effectiveness states that once a group's membership rises above _____, communication tends to become focused within a few members.

    A. 3   B. 5   C. 7   D. 9

2. Which of the following is a reason why management may want to centralize authority in an organization?

    A. Encouraging the development of professional managers
    B. Avoiding duplication of functions
    C. Encouraging competitiveness in the organization
    D. Discouraging managerial delegation

3. Which of the following is a process theory of motivation?

    A. E-R-G model
    B. Two-factor model
    C. Organizational behavior modification
    D. Maslow's hierarchy of needs

4. Which of the following organizational decisions is in line with the idea of centralization?

    A. Product departments   B. Delegated authority
    C. Wide spans of control   D. Low specialization

5. Committees within an organization often create special human problems, most likely because

    A. people are unable to get along with outsiders
    B. people are unable to make adjustments from their normal work roles and relationships
    C. lines of authority are not clearly drawn
    D. it is difficult to agree on the nature of problems

6. Which of the following is considered to be a direct cause of group productivity?

    A. Member motivation   B. Norms
    C. Group size   D. Group cohesiveness

7. In general, people tend to pay attention to those features of their work environment which are consistent with or which reinforce their own expectations. This phenomena is known as

    A. adverse selection   B. ethnocentrism
    C. individualization   D. selective perception

8. Within an organization, a supervisor's span of control is LEAST likely to depend on the

   A. rate of change in the organization
   B. ability of the supervisor to delegate work to others
   C. number of potential relationships
   D. amount of personal contact between employees

9. What is the term for a mental state of anxiety that occurs when there's a conflict among a person's attitudes and beliefs after a decision has been made?

   A. Paradox
   B. Cognitive dissonance
   C. Situational assonance
   D. Paranoia

10. In the non-verbal communication process, meaning is most commonly provided by

    A. body language
    B. symbols
    C. words
    D. context

11. The general consensus about quality circles is that when they are used, the ideal size is _____ members.

    A. 4   B. 8   C. 11   D. 15

12. The safety department of an organization makes three safety checks a year in each department, on a random basis. According to the theory of organizational behavior modification, the department is practicing a _____ schedule of behavioral reinforcement.

    A. variable interval
    B. fixed interval
    C. variable ratio
    D. fixed ratio

13. In organizational decision-making, the alternative outcome relationship is based on each of the following possible conditions EXCEPT

    A. risk
    B. certainty
    C. feasibility
    D. uncertainty

14. In job design, which of the following is a way for management to increase an employee's core job dimensions?

    A. Separating task elements
    B. Opening feedback channels
    C. Assigning smaller fragments of work
    D. Clearly delineating work methods to be used

15. In order to achieve the maximum benefits of bureaucratic design in an organization,

    A. employment should be based on technical qualifications
    B. tasks should be divided along generalized lines
    C. employees should relate in an informal, personal manner
    D. members or offices should report to more than one manager

16. During planned change in an organization, the *unfreezing* situation is characterized by each of the following EXCEPT

   A. the linking of rewards with a willingness to change
   B. the strengthening of social supports
   C. experiences designed to help individuals see a current routine as less attractive
   D. the physical removal of the individual or group being changed from accustomed routines

17. *Theory X* of human behavior can be described as a(n)

   A. model that adapts the elements of Japanese management systems to the U.S. organizational culture
   B. humanistic and supportive set of assumptions
   C. approach to management that emphasizes cooperation and interdependence
   D. autocratic and traditional set of assumptions

18. In the theory and practice of contingency design, environmental factors are divided into subenvironments which influence the structure of an organization. Which of the following is not a type of subenvironment?

   A. Technical   B. Market
   C. Strategic   D. Production

19. The practice of allowing employees to perform a complete piece of work is commonly referred to as

   A. job enlargement   B. modulation
   C. task identity   D. positive reinforcement

20. Which of the following is considered to be a social leadership role in groups?

   A. Evaluating the group's effectiveness
   B. Summarizing the discussion
   C. Determining whether agreement has been reached
   D. Requesting facts, ideas, or opinions from members

21. Which of the following is described as a *primary* individual need?

   A. Sense of duty   B. Competitiveness
   C. Safety   D. Self-esteem

22. Which of the following is TRUE of an organization with an organic structure?

   A. Motivation taps physical, security, and economic motives
   B. Performance goals are low and passively sought
   C. Information flows upward, downward, and laterally
   D. Interaction is closed and restricted

23. Which of the following is NOT generally considered to be a necessary prerequisite for the job redesign process?

    A. Securing the involvement of unions
    B. Determining the exact size of the necessary workforce
    C. Making changes in the work itself
    D. Using monetary rewards

24. In Fiedler's contingency model of leadership, a structured leader is most likely to be effective in a position of _____ power, _____ task structure, and _____ leader member relations.

    A. weak; high; moderately good
    B. high; high; good
    C. weak; low; poor
    D. high; low; good

25. Each of the following is generally considered to be a logical, rational reason for an employee who resists change in the organization EXCEPT the

    A. economical costs of change
    B. need for security
    C. extra effort required to relearn
    D. technical feasibility of change

KEY (CORRECT ANSWERS)

1.	C	11.	B
2.	B	12.	A
3.	C	13.	C
4.	C	14.	B
5.	B	15.	A
6.	A	16.	B
7.	D	17.	D
8.	C	18.	C
9.	B	19.	C
10.	A	20.	A

21. C
22. C
23. B
24. C
25. B

TEST 2

DIRECTIONS: Each question or incomplete statement is followed by several suggested answers or completions. Select the one that BEST answers the question or completes the statement. *PRINT THE LETTER OF THE CORRECT ANSWER IN THE SPACE AT THE RIGHT.*

1. Which of the following is TRUE of formal organizations?

    A. Within them, behavior is governed by sanctions.
    B. Their leaders' power is granted by the group.
    C. Their primary focus is on people, rather than positions.
    D. Their major concepts are authority and responsibility.

2. Which of the following steps in the two-way communication process occurs LAST?

    A. Using
    B. Decoding
    C. Accepting
    D. Providing feedback

3. Which of the following is considered to be a potential disadvantage associated with the Delphi decision-making process?

    A. Inadequate time for reflection
    B. Few opportunities for interaction between panelists
    C. Inefficient uses of experts' time
    D. Interpersonal problems among panelists

4. A person's attitudes are considered to be composed of each of the following EXCEPT

    A. experiences
    B. intentions to act
    C. feelings
    D. thoughts

5. Which of the following is another term for product departmentalization?

    A. Horizontal specialization
    B. Divisional organization
    C. Categorical compartmentalization
    D. Vertical integration

6. Oldham's job characteristics model suggests that there are critical psychological states which are crucial in determining a person's motivation and job satisfaction. Which of the following is NOT one of these?

    A. Knowledge
    B. Responsibility
    C. Meaningfulness
    D. Satisfaction

7. The principal advantage of using functional departmentalization within an organization is

    A. provision of an ideal training ground for new workers
    B. clear priority of organizational goals over departmental goals
    C. easier expansion into new geographic areas
    D. efficiency

8. Which of the following reports or statistics relating to stress in U.S. organizations is inaccurate or false?

    A. 70 percent of workers report that stress-related health problems have made them less productive.
    B. 30 percent of executives believe their work has adversely affected their health.
    C. The annual cost of stress-related absenteeism, lower productivity, rising health insurance costs, and other medical expenses is now somewhere near $100 million.
    D. Stress-related workers' compensation claims have tripled in the last decade, jumping from 5 percent to 15 percent of all claims.

9. What is the term for the cyclical process of identifying system problems, gathering data, taking corrective action, and making ongoing adjustments?

    A. Consultative management
    B. Affirmative action
    C. Double-loop learning
    D. Action research

10. Symptoms of *burnout* on the job do NOT typically include

    A. a feeling of inability to accomplish goals
    B. emotional exhaustion
    C. chronic worry
    D. a feeling of detachment from clients and work

11. What is the term for the process of reducing a communication to a few basic details that can be remembered and passed on to others?

    A. Filtering
    B. Seep
    C. Distorting
    D. Distilling

12. _____ personality theories are based on the premise that predispositions direct the behavior of an individual in a consistent pattern.

    A. Psychodynamic
    B. Behavioral
    C. Trait
    D. Humanistic

13. Each of the following is a commonly used method for encouraging upward communication within organizations EXCEPT

    A. employee meetings
    B. open-door policies
    C. grievance systems
    D. suggestion screening

14. According to Likert's organization development approach, which of the following is/are intervening variables?

    A. Attitudes
    B. Leadership behavior
    C. Organizational structure
    D. Customer loyalty

15. Of the following, which is NOT a type of barrier to effective communication? 15.____

    A. Personal   B. Semantic   C. Syntactic   D. Physical

16. Which of the following is the proponent of the two-factor model of motivation? 16.____

    A. Vroom   B. Alderfer
    C. Hertzberg   D. Maslow

17. Which of the following is a perceptual defect which causes a person to attribute his or her own characteristics and feelings to others? 17.____

    A. Projection
    B. Self-serving bias
    C. Fundamental attribution bias
    D. Stereotyping

18. Each of the following behaviors is considered to be a part of a leader's *coaching* role in an organization EXCEPT 18.____

    A. listening to employee input
    B. personally participating in work tasks
    C. selecting the appropriate personnel for tasks
    D. reviewing resource needs

19. Which of the following is a procedure that is generally observed by nominal groups? 19.____

    A. Group members individually designate their preferences for alternatives by secret ballot.
    B. Ideas are shared with others in an open, non-structured format.
    C. Group members develop solutions cooperatively, in discussion.
    D. Several periods of time are allotted for questioning.

20. Which of the following is LEAST likely to be a cause of stress on the job? 20.____

    A. Differences in company values and employee values
    B. Time pressures
    C. Narrowly-defined roles
    D. Work overload

21. Most often, the rationale for grouping jobs in an organization rests on 21.____

    A. the necessity for coordinating them
    B. the existing formal hierarchy
    C. the need for lines of communication
    D. industry standards

22. According to the performance model, potential performance is a product of 22.____

    A. motivation and experience
    B. ability and motivation
    C. satisfaction and ability
    D. ability and experience

23. In terms of organizational structure, it has become standard practice to use the term _____ to refer to the number of different units at the same level.

    A. boundary division
    B. formalization
    C. horizontal differentiation
    D. vertical differentiation

24. In nondirective counseling that occurs in the workplace, an emphasis is generally placed on

    A. psychological adjustment
    B. social integration
    C. solution of current problems
    D. individual performance

25. In the path-goal model of leadership, which of the following steps is typically performed FIRST?

    A. Appropriate goals are established.
    B. Leader connects rewards with goals.
    C. Leader provides assistance.
    D. Leader identifies employee needs.

KEY (CORRECT ANSWERS)

1.	D	11.	A
2.	D	12.	C
3.	B	13.	D
4.	A	14.	A
5.	B	15.	C
6.	D	16.	C
7.	D	17.	A
8.	C	18.	B
9.	D	19.	A
10.	C	20.	C

21. A
22. B
23. C
24. A
25. D

EXAMINATION SECTION
TEST 1

DIRECTIONS: Each question or incomplete statement is followed by several suggested answers or completions. Select the one that BEST answers the question or completes the statement. *PRINT THE LETTER OF THE CORRECT ANSWER IN THE SPACE AT THE RIGHT.*

1. An individual incentive plan where pay fluctuates based on units of production per time period is described as

    A. red circle
    B. standard-hour
    C. differential piece rate
    D. straight piecework

    1.____

2. In the experience of most employees, which of the following career stages lasts approximately from age 30 to 45?

    A. Midcareer crisis
    B. Advancement
    C. Maintenance
    D. Establishment

    2.____

3. Which of the following statements about effective leadership is generally NOT accepted by human resource managers?

    A. Employees often expect a supervisor to structure their behavior.
    B. A combination of high-supportive and high-directive styles is often a successful leadership style.
    C. Higher management will often set preferences regarding the leadership styles of lower-level managers and supervisors.
    D. Under emergency or high-pressure situations, emphasis on personal well-being is desirable and often preferred by employees.

    3.____

4. The Employment Retirement Income Security Act (ERISA), as amended, limits the eligibility requirements that an employer may establish for receiving retirement benefits. Specifically, an employer is prohibited from establishing a requirement of more than _____ of service.

    A. six months
    B. one year
    C. 3 years
    D. 5 years

    4.____

5. In a company's compensation policy, the most significant factor determining the company's external competitiveness is/are its

    A. benefits
    B. mix of various forms of pay
    C. career opportunities
    D. level of pay

    5.____

6. In an organization with a human resources department, which of the following information is most likely to be covered by the human resources manager in orienting a new employee?

    A. Introducing the new employee to other employees in the work unit
    B. Communicating the objectives and philosophy of the organization

    6.____

C. Discussing policies on performance and conduct
D. Familiarizing the employee with the physical work environment

7. The Age Discrimination in Employment Act of 1968 prohibits discrimination against individuals who are over _____ years of age.

   A. 30 B. 40 C. 50 D. 60

8. Which of the following types of personnel are most likely to be recruited with the assistance of private employment agencies?

   A. Commissioned sales
   B. Office/clerical
   C. Production/service
   D. Managers/supervisors

9. Advocates of hierarchical pay structures believe

   A. equal treatment will result in more knowledgeable employees going unrewarded and unrecognized
   B. all employees in an organization have an equal number of compensable factors
   C. managers should by virtue of their position earn more than line workers
   D. seniority should be the primary factor on which pay is based

10. In designing a training program for employees, it is important to remember that usually the first stage of learning is described as

    A. behavioral
    B. cognitive
    C. performance alteration
    D. experimental

11. In a(n) _____ situation, all employees pay union dues whether or not they are union members.

    A. decertified
    B. agency shop
    C. craft union
    D. collective bargaining

12. In the employee training process, which of the following tasks is most likely to be jointly undertaken by both the human resources manager and the operating manager?

    A. Selecting the trainer
    B. Developing training criteria
    C. Doing the training
    D. Evaluating the training

13. In behavioral theory, a decline in the rate of a behavior that is brought about by nonreinforcement is known as

    A. extinction
    B. norming
    C. regression
    D. conformity

14. Of all the relationships between performance evaluation and other personnel management activities, the most critical to understand today is the relationship between evaluation and

    A. human resources research
    B. equal employment opportunity
    C. motivation
    D. productivity

15. The main disadvantage of the *hot stove* method of employee discipline is that 15.____

    A. its benefits are more long-term than immediate
    B. it fails to recognize individual and situational differences
    C. it invites personal bias on the part of the manager
    D. does not allow for detailed recordkeeping

16. Today, the average employer can be expected to pay about _____ a year or more per employee for benefits. 16.____

    A. $1,000   B. $5,000   C. $9,000   D. $12,000

17. Supervised training and testing for a minimum time period, until an employee has acquired a minimum skill level, is commonly referred to as 17.____

    A. apprenticeship training   B. vestibule training
    C. on-the-job training   D. programmed instruction

18. Most human resource professionals believe that the most effective approach to on-the-job training for managers involves 18.____

    A. a mix of transfers (to new geographic locations) and rotations through jobs
    B. mentoring
    C. vestibule training
    D. coaching and counseling, coupled with a structured rotation through jobs and functions

19. The motivation-maintenance theory of employee management deals primarily with motivation through 19.____

    A. job design   B. collegiality
    C. behavioral modification   D. external rewards

20. In what year did the American Federation of Labor (AFL) merge with the Congress of Industrial Organizations (CIO)? 20.____

    A. 1886   B. 1938   C. 1955   D. 1966

21. Which of the following is a *critical-incident* system for rating employees? 21.____

    A. Alteration ranking
    B. Behavioral observation scale (BOS)
    C. Classification
    D. Forced-choice rating

22. Likely pitfalls to management by objectives (MBO) include each of the following EXCEPT 22.____

    A. too much emphasis on the long term
    B. failure to tie MBO results with rewards
    C. too much paperwork
    D. setting too many objectives

23. Typically, organizations that implement group incentive programs are most likely to use _____ as the basis for group pay.

    A. customer satisfaction
    B. quality
    C. financial measures
    D. productivity measures (output to input ratios)

24. Which of the following skills is most likely to be taught in training programs at a U.S. organization?

    A. Computer skills   B. Clerical skills
    C. Executive development D. Customer relations

25. If an employer is found guilty, upon inspection by OSHA, of a serious violation of the federal health and safety code, and it is found that the violation is negligent rather than willful, the penalty is typically

    A. $1,000 per citation
    B. $10,000 per citation
    C. $10,000 or up to six months in jail
    D. $10,000 and/or six months in jail

KEY (CORRECT ANSWERS)

1.	D	11.	B
2.	B	12.	A
3.	D	13.	A
4.	B	14.	B
5.	D	15.	B
6.	B	16.	C
7.	B	17.	A
8.	D	18.	D
9.	A	19.	A
10.	B	20.	C

21.	B
22.	A
23.	C
24.	A
25.	A

TEST 2

DIRECTIONS: Each question or incomplete statement is followed by several suggested answers or completions. Select the one that BEST answers the question or completes the statement. *PRINT THE LETTER OF THE CORRECT ANSWER IN THE SPACE AT THE RIGHT.*

1. Which of the following statements about employment agencies and executive search firms is/are TRUE?
    I. Most employment agencies work on retainer.
    II. Executive agencies are paid only when they have actually provided a new hire.
    III. Executive search firms generally do a better job of maintaining confidentiality.
    The CORRECT answer is:

    A. I only   B. I, II   C. III only   D. I, II, III

    1._____

2. _____ is a training method in which, after material is presented in text form, a trainee is required to read and answer questions relating to the text.

    A. Cross-training
    B. Programmed instruction
    C. Apprenticeship training
    D. Classroom training

    2._____

3. In the training process, which of the following is most likely to be done by the operating manager?

    A. Doing the training
    B. Developing training criteria
    C. Determining training needs and objectives
    D. Developing training material

    3._____

4. The purpose of a market pay line is to

    A. pull the wages of competitors upward
    B. determine the maximum total payroll needed to maintain profit and productivity
    C. discourage the formation of a labor union
    D. summarize the pay rates of various jobs in the labor market

    4._____

5. When selection procedures at an organization involve the use of tests to measure leadership characteristics and/or personality, tests with _____ validity are generally most appropriate.

    A. construct
    B. content
    C. alternate-form
    D. criterion-related

    5._____

6. Which of the following is NOT a typical disadvantage associated with variable pay plans? Employees

    A. are unable to minimize risk through diversification
    B. may be likely to intentionally decrease their individual effort
    C. tend to count on bonus pay regardless of the likelihood of receiving it
    D. may feel penalized for factors beyond their control

    6._____

7. Which of the following is an employee rating method, using 6 to 10 performance dimensions, that uses critical incidents as anchor statements placed along a scale?

    A. Forced-choice rating
    B. Behaviorally anchored rating scale (BARS)
    C. Forced-distribution rating
    D. Behavioral observation scale (BOS)

8. Many organizations today provide an alternative to traditional career pathing, and base career paths on real-world experiences and individualized preferences. Paths of this kind typically have each of the following characteristics EXCEPT

    A. they are definite and remain stable when organizational needs change
    B. they include lateral and downward possibilities
    C. each job along the path is specified in terms of acquirable skills and knowledge rather than merely educational credentials or work experience
    D. they are flexible enough to take individual qualities into account

9. Title VI of the 1964 Civil Rights Act prohibits discrimination based on several characteristics in all programs or activities that receive federal financial aid in order to provide employment. Which of the following types of discrimination is NOT explicitly outlawed by this law?

    A. Race
    B. Sex
    C. Color
    D. National origin

10. Which of the following types of organizations is exempt from the provisions of the Occupational Safety and Health Act?

    A. Businesses employing 15 or fewer people
    B. Government contractors for projects whose costs total less than $50,000
    C. Businesses employing only family members
    D. Businesses in non-industrial service sectors

11. Which of the following is not a legally mandated employee benefit?

    A. Family leave
    B. Unemployment compensation
    C. Worker's compensation
    D. Child care

12. Human resource planning is LEAST likely to be important if the goals of top management include

    A. rapid expansion
    B. merging
    C. stable growth
    D. diversification

13. _____ is the process of grouping personnel activities into related work units.

    A. Apportionment
    B. Allotment
    C. Blocking
    D. Departmentation

14. Of the following criteria used in the selection process, which is most potentially troublesome in light of equal employment opportunity laws?

    A. Personal characteristics
    B. Physical characteristics
    C. Experience/past performance
    D. Formal education

15. Each of the following is generally true of a laissez-faire leader and the group in his or her charge EXCEPT

    A. decisions are typically made by whoever is willing to make them
    B. morale is low
    C. individuals have little interest in their work
    D. the leader is very conscious of his or her position

16. A work situation in which a union is not present and there is no management effort to keep a union out is known as a(n) _____ shop.

    A. preferential   B. open
    C. restricted   D. closed

17. In a job evaluation that is conducted using the point method, which of the following would typically be performed FIRST?

    A. Preparing job descriptions
    B. Choosing compensable factors
    C. Establishing factor scales
    D. Conducting job analysis

18. The Pregnancy Discrimination Act requires employers to

    A. allow up to twelve weeks of leave for birth or adoption
    B. ask job candidates whether they are pregnant
    C. not consider pregnancy to be a disability
    D. treat pregnancy just like any other medical condition with regard to fringe benefits and leave policies

19. An agreement between an employee and management, that, as a condition of employment, the employee will not join a labor union, is known as a _____ contract.

    A. wildcat   B. zero-tolerance
    C. yellow-dog   D. submission

20. Effective human resource departments distinguish between employee training as an ongoing activity and training as a strategic tool for attaining the goals of the organization and the employees. In general, training for specific, measurable impact is characterized by a

    A. programmed sequence based on existing programs
    B. training environment that is separate from the work environment
    C. partnership with the client
    D. link to a philosophy rather than a business need

21. Which of the following statements about comparable worth is FALSE? 21.____
    It

    A. is the principal method suggested to reduce the earnings gap between men and women
    B. provides a plan for racial equity in the labor market
    C. allows external market concerns to dominate internal equity
    D. focuses on pay differences among different occupations

22. The use of employee referrals is sometimes a powerful personnel recruitment technique, but it has the important potential disadvantage of 22.____

    A. fostering jealousy and resentment among employees
    B. taking some decision-making powers away from management
    C. discouraging a shared sense of responsibility
    D. risking accidental violation of equal employment opportunity laws

23. When labor and management are in conflict on an issue, and when the outcome is a win/lose situation, _____ is said to be occurring. 23.____

    A. distributive bargaining   B. forced-choice ranking
    C. integrative bargaining   D. collective bargaining

24. Human resource managers sometimes deal with employee surpluses by encouraging attrition. The main potential disadvantage associated with this approach is that it 24.____

    A. involves costly severance packages
    B. can amount to layoffs of older employees
    C. occurs too slowly to be considered responsive to current surpluses
    D. discourages new ideas and experimentation from younger employees

25. In which of the following industries is the highest percentage of workers represented by unions? 25.____

    A. Manufacturing   B. Construction
    C. Wholesale/retail trade   D. Government workers

KEY (CORRECT ANSWERS)

1. C
2. B
3. A
4. D
5. A

6. B
7. B
8. A
9. B
10. C

11. D
12. C
13. D
14. B
15. D

16. B
17. D
18. D
19. C
20. C

21. C
22. D
23. A
24. B
25. D

TECHNIQUES OF DECISION MAKING

CONTENTS

INSTRUCTIONAL OBJECTIVES		1
CONTENT		1
Introduction		1
1.	What is Decision Making?	
2.	A Formula for Decision Making	2
A.	Isolate the Problem	3
	What Is the Real Problem?	
	What Are the Problems?	
	What Are the Symptoms?	
B.	Analyze the Facts	5
	How Many Facts Should be Gathered?	
	Where Are the Needed Facts Obtained?	
C.	Organizing the Facts	7
	Grouping the Facts	
	Cost	
	Time	
	Past Precedent	
	Procedure	
	Leadership	
	Quality	
	Productivity	
D.	Stating the Real Problem	9
	Is There a Real Problem or Just Symptoms?	
	What Objective Is To Be Achieved?	
E.	Developing Alternative Solutions	10
	Present All Alternatives for Consideration	
	List the Alternatives	
F.	Selecting the Best Alternative Solution	11
	List the Consequences of the Decision	
	Be a Devil's Advocate	
	Scrutinize the Final Alternatives Thoroughly	
	Involve Your Superiors	
G.	Implement the Decision	13
3.	Summation	13
STUDENT LEARNING ACTIVITIES		14
TEACHER MANAGEMENT ACTIVITIES		15
EVALUATION QUESTIONS		17

TECHNIQUES OF DECISION MAKING

INSTRUCTIONAL OBJECTIVES

1. Ability to define decision making.
2. Ability to learn the decision-making formula.
3. Ability to learn how to state problems simply and accurately.
4. Ability to determine the difference between a symptom and a cause.
5. Ability to determine which facts are most important to a decision.
6. Ability to be able to qualify information according to importance and subject classification.
7. Ability to learn to identify two or more alternative solutions for a problem.
8. Ability to develop an openness to creative ideas.
9. Ability to learn to weigh the consequences of alternative decisions.
10. Ability to select and justify the most appropriate decision.

CONTENT

INTRODUCTION

Every person, each day, is faced by numerous situations which require the making of many decisions throughout the course of the day. It is necessary to answer such questions as: *When do I get up in the morning? What clothes will I wear? What will I have for breakfast? Which route will I take to school?*

Working in the field of public service, an individual is constantly faced with a series of situations which require him to take some particular course of action. Many such actions may not require special decision making on his part, because his particular organization has provided ways for him to make these decisions rather automatically. For example, there are department policies, and standard ways of performing certain jobs. A person also has his own past experiences of success which enable him to easily make certain decisions for such things as: the hours he should work, his rate of pay, and the required forms which must be completed for certain kinds of activities. All of these things are handled rather automatically on the job, because people have methods of handling certain things in certain ways. These become habit. They fit within a regular pattern.

There are many situations faced by a decision maker where the consequences of his action are so minor that it doesn't really matter which way he decides to solve a given problem as long as it is resolved: for example, what pencil to choose; the color of the paper on a final report; the diverting of automobiles during a traffic jam.

However, there are also other situations where the way a manager or supervisor solves a problem has great impact on an organization. Sometimes a person doesn't have a chance to actually know what is right and what is wrong. Judgment might have no well established basis. The opportunity to select between two alternatives of equal value does not exist. The situation is not clearcut. It requires thought and careful judgment; it has far-reaching consequences on the organization-affecting the quality of service, costs, schedules, the relationships between people in a working unit. Appropriate action must be taken in such assorted areas as overtime, employee dismissal, grievances, types of equipment to purchase, ways to reduce waste. The effectiveness and efficiency of the decision-making process of one individual can have far-reaching impact on a public-service organization.

Good decisions allow individuals to control and monitor their operations. Bad ones can cause worse problems and hinder the effectiveness of an organization. Things just don't happen by chance. They are made to happen. They are arranged. They can quite often be developed over a period of time which has been required by the nature of the problem or activity.

1. <u>WHAT IS DECISION MAKING?</u>

Decision making involves a conscious choice or selection of one behavior alternative from a group of two or more behavior alternatives.

Thus, there are two basic elements in a decision-making process: one, the matter of conscious choice, and the other of alternatives. *To decide, then, really means to cut off, to come to a conclusion, to end.*

2. <u>*A FORMULA FOR DECISION MAKING*</u>

Decision-making is a skill that can be developed. One way in which it can be developed is through a formula, a procedure which provides a formal process or system involving the basic rules of decision-making. There are no born decision makers, but some people appear to act very efficiently on the basis of hunches. These people may never be seen with charts and graphs, or performing a lot of analytical tasks. However, they've probably developed their own way of sifting facts and of solving problems. Good decision makers usually know their personnel; have prior experience; they can put together difficult possibilities quickly. They have their own personal *formulas* of decision making.

An effective technique to help make decisions is through the aid of a formula – a kind of check-off list to help find answers to difficult situations, to resolve problems, to handle unique situations. Such a formula enables one to take advantage of his past experiences, to see the whole picture, and to utilize all the facts he can find which are applicable to the solution.

A decision-making formula worthy of our consideration has six steps:

- *Isolate* - State the apparent problem or situation with which you plan to deal.

- *Analyze* - Gather the facts.

- *Diagnose* - Organize and interpret the facts.

- *Prescribe procedures* - State the real problem or situation.

- *Implement procedures* - Develop alternative solutions.

- *Evaluate* - Select the most appropriate alternative. Decide.

We will consider each of these steps separately. However, it should be kept in mind that these separate steps are really all related and part of the whole process of decision making.

A. *Isolate the Problem*. A problem can be a situation, question, matter, or person that is perplexing or difficult, that obstructs the way to achieving a goal or objective.

Almost everyone has problems: students have study problems when they don't know answers to test questions; people have money problems when they can't pay all of their bills. Individuals have problems with people who are unfriendly; problems with their girlfriends or boyfriends; growth problems; health problems; psychological problems.

There are professionals and specialists to whom people can go with their problems. A person takes his malfunctioning car to a mechanic, he calls on the plumber to fix leaky pipes, contacts the doctor when he doesn't feel well. These specialists are skilled problem solvers in a particular area. They have had special training and experience. They may even have had to pass examinations to obtain certificates or licenses.

In decision making, one must recognize problems as well as symptoms of problems. It is particularly important to be able to separate symptoms from causes.

What is the Real Problem? Problems are often presented in very broad terms: "Gee, John, they've really fouled up in accounting. Go straighten them out." "Boy, do we have a morale problem." "We have to introduce that new system right away." "Those two managers just don't get along."

Consider the question of morale, for example. Is morale really the problem, or is it more accurately the symptom of another problem? Chances are that it is a symptom of a problem rather than the real problem itself. The problem situation might be poor organizational structure, bad working conditions, an unfriendly supervisor, unfair treatment, or a number of other difficulties.

To help in determining what is a symptom and what is a cause, several questions must be asked:

- *"How else might the problem be stated?"* The placement of accountants in one isolated department, without the opportunity to discuss actual income and outgo with supervisors, has given us unrealistic budget figures.

  The lack of adding machines, a broken calculator, dim light, uncomfortable room temperatures, and individual working spaces has caused a greater number of absences.

  The accounting manager has openly criticized senior staff members in front of their fellow workers.

  The department secretaries were all forced to work overtime for staying five minutes past their lunch hours.

- *"What else is involved?"*

  If there are no communications between accountants and supervisors, neither group will know the reasons behind the requests or needs of the others.

  There has been talk about a computer eliminating some of the accounting jobs.

  The senior accountants have been slow to pick up the new accounting procedures.

  This is the tenth time this month that the financial unit has been unable to take care of the people in line because the secretaries were not here.

- *"Are there similar problems in other departments?"*

  The people in supplies have been ordering the wrong equipment.

  There have been layoffs in several departments.

  Several department managers are competing for the job of assistant director of our organization.

  None of the other departments have problems with secretaries.

- *"Is this a problem or a symptom?"*

    The real problem is that the accountants have not been properly informed of the organizational structure, and thus have very poor understanding of the departments which comprise the organization.

    Another organization nearby has announced opportunities for accountants at higher pay, and in new offices.

    The accounting manager and his senior staff do not plan departmental modifications together.

    Only one of the secretaries has a watch and it is five minutes slow. They play bridge at lunch time several days each month.

- *"How do others perceive the problem?"*

    Talk to all the accountants and managers individually.

    Talk to personnel about accounting re-classification.

    Interview the senior staff.

Visit with the secretaries.

<u>What are the Problems? What are the Symptoms?</u> If your automobile won't start, it might not be because it's old, the engine is dirty, or your windshield wipers don't work the car may be out of gas. It might, however, be time to give it some other attention, too. If you can recognize the symptoms, you can avoid a lot of problems.

B. <u>Analyze the Facts.</u> When the problem is recognized, then all the facts required for a successful decision can, and should be accumulated. Too often, people think they have all the facts, but they don't. It's like trying to put together a jigsaw puzzle, and recognizing, after many frustrating hours, that six pieces are missing.

   Frequently, the decision maker feels that because he is in a particular situation, he knows it better than anyone else can know it. The issue may, therefore, be somewhat clouded. This cloudiness may prevent him from seeing what is actually there.

   How many times have individuals had to make a decision and found that they didn't have the right facts or sufficient quantities of facts to insure a good decision? Both the quality and effectiveness of most decisions can be seriously reduced without good facts.

   When gathering facts, one should write them down, and gather them into one comprehensive list. The decision maker can then visualize them all at the same time, and is much less likely to overlook or forget any of them. In dealing with large amounts of information, he can grade sub-topics and keep track of them in a systematic way.

How many facts should be gathered? The number usually depends on the nature and complexity of the situation.

Basically it means that the amount of information accumulated depends upon such factors as:

- The amount of time available.
- Is it an emergency situation or not?
- The seriousness of the situation.
- The availability of information, etc.

Where are the Needed Facts Obtained?

- First, he might turn to available records. He usually has financial records, personal records, records of transactions, and records of activities.
- Second, he may have references: newspapers, journals, old letters, the like.
- Third, and very importantly, he has other people, or he has a staff. There is a great deal of expertise within most public-service organizations: specialists in economics, human relations, law, health, safety, and other areas; all responsive to the request of the decision-maker. An outside expert, or consultant, may be required in difficult situations.
- Finally, look at other organizational units which have been confronted with similar problems. Quite often, through investigation, the decision-maker finds that precedents have been set which he may have to follow. In law, for example, he may have to base a decis.ion on the verdict of a case held on the same issue, long ago in a distant place.

Sources of information are unlimited. It takes a great deal of initiative to uncover them.

How should the facts be obtained? Here again, there are questions we must ask ourselves:

- What kinds of facts are available?
- What information is available?
- Is there enough?

- Is help needed, and where can it be obtained?
- Who else might have the information needed?

Going back to the morale problem, which was found to be the result of a basic lack of communication between accountants and departmental managers, how might the decision-maker proceed?

In gathering the facts, he would have to obtain both the accountant's records and the manager's records. The decision-maker might call upon organizations of similar size and activity, to see how they handle difficulties of this nature. He might talk to one or more senior accountants in a large public accounting firm or contact the governmental auditors. He might even write letters to colleagues seeking their advice.

The decision-maker might hold a meeting of selected members of his staff, or assign a task force of accountants and managers to look into the matter.

As he begins to gather his facts, the decision-maker will discover that other information is required. Additionally, he will uncover sources of other facts. The quality of the facts he gathers ultimately affects the quality of his decisions. The better the data, the better the opportunity to make a good decision.

C. Organizing the Facts. Once the facts have been collected, it becomes very important that they be organized to help the decision-maker interpret what they really mean. To do this, it's helpful to set them up in categories -- to pull like items together.

This procedure helps people to know whether certain facts are more important than others, and thus deserve special consideration.

Grouping the Facts. There are several categories into which information can be grouped, such as: cost, time, past precedent, procedures, leadership, quality, and productivity:

Cost. In cost considerations, one must look at unit costs, personnel costs, material costs, equipment costs, mailing costs, etc. If, for example, an individual is attempting to determine the cost of mailing out new contracts to several hundred vendors with whom the agency deals, the following costs may have to be considered, among others:

- *Duplication costs per duplicated copy.*
- *Salary costs of writing new contract.*
- *Salary costs of typing contracts.*
- *Costs of new contract forms.*

- *Costs of envelopes.*
- *Costs of writing departmental letters.*

Time. Time is usually calculated in terms of the personnel costs or salaries paid. The basic periods of time hours, days, weeks, months, years are quite often combined in terms of man-hours, man-weeks, man-years, etc., to enable the numbers of hour units to be multiplied by salary allocations. Equipment time, particularly in this age of computers, can be quite expensive.

Past Precedent. This is a category relating together data on similar situations in the past, and to consider the decisions arrived at in those situations for their bearing on the decision to be made in the present.

Procedures. These are also important. Most public-service organizations have certain ways of accomplishing functions or providing services. They have been proven over a period of time to be most appropriate to particular situations. Here, too, is where organizational policy making may be involved and possibly changed and modified.

Leadership. This would include the directions and decisions which brought about a particular situation, and permit review of the factors which were present when prior decisions were made.

Quality. The quality of facts is important. There must be an assurance that the right data, and the most applicable figures and information, are available.

Productivity. This category would enable a comparison between various activities which would bring about particular results. It would provide an opportunity to look at the output of a department or project team.

In pulling together like items, one can see trends, certain facts which may be more important than others, and areas where there are gaps in the information.

In organizing facts, the following questions should be asked:

- Which facts are related to each other?
- Are these facts related to any not listed?
- What is the extent of their relationship?
- Are they relevant to this situation?
- What is the level of reliability of the facts?
- Can the problem be more clearly defined with the information listed?

- How can it be done?

- How much time is there for further organization?

- Are these facts recurring or one time events?

D. *Stating the Real Problem.* Having examined the data, the decision-maker is now in a position to state the *real* problem or situation with which he has to deal. He now knows whether he has a problem, or just a misunderstanding. Was the original statement just a symptom, or was it a real situation? It might be that there are several problems. Whatever the situation, it must be stated in clear and simple terms. It should be written down.

A problem is a situation which deviates from an expected standard, or norm of desired performance. In decision making, one starts with an *apparent* problem. The decision maker gathers more information in order to more accurately identify the situation with which he is going to deal.

Is there a real problem? or just symptoms? The data have been gathered and organized. Now it is necessary to zero in on the actual situation, and to see whether there is a real problem. Was the initial identification a symptom of a problem, or was it a real cause? Is there one problem, or several?

If the decision-maker neglected to gather the facts, and then to organize, analyze, and categorize them, he might find himself working on the wrong situation. He could spend a great deal of time and effort on symptoms, and could actually be working on the wrong problem. Certainly, he could overlook a number of relevant factors.

If a medical doctor spent all of his time studying symptoms, he might be too late to address an actual problem and his patient could die. Similarly, in a public-service organization, *if too much time and energy is spent in chasing symptoms instead of causes, problems can become crises.*

What objective is to be achieved? Remember, one must still think about decision making in terms of fulfilling objectives.

When it is known what kind of performance should be achieved, and what kind of performance has been received, the necessary effort is simple merely to measure the difference between those two points. The decision-maker must identify the deviation and its extent. He will also have to specifically state the standard, or *norm,* toward which he is trying to return.

In other words, not only does he have to state the problem to which he is going to address himself, but he must specifically state the objective he wants to achieve.

In the previous illustration of the public-service organization and the communication problems between the accountants and managers, the objectives could, perhaps, be restated in this manner: *it is necessary to design a realistic and accurate budget for costs.*

This stage would complete the problem identification part of the decision-making process. Now, he can get on with decision-making itself.

E. *Developing Alternative Solutions.* With the *real* problem determined and stated, the decision-maker is now in a position to begin the development of alternative solutions. Notice that there is an "s" on the end of "solution." Decision-makers should be interested in as many solutions to a problem as can be developed.

This particular phase of the decision making process should be very free-wheeling. It should produce a number of ideas. The decision-maker should keep his mind open. He should not be too judgmental, but should avoid premature criticism. *Criticism given too early can destroy new ideas that could be beneficial.*

Picture a staff meeting, where the assistant director of the agency presents an entirely new approach to providing recreational opportunities for senior citizens. He is interrupted by his superior, the director, who tells him that his idea is ridiculous. It is unlikely that he would ever bring up the subject again unless he were extremely persistent and unafraid of the director. *Creative thinking can be squelched by a superior who criticizes without having much of a basis for criticism.*

The number of alternatives that can be developed at any one point in time is a function of how much time is spent in developing these alternatives. It's always helpful to stop and ask: "If I didn't have any rules to follow in this organization, would I handle the situation any differently?" Or, "What else could I do?" Perhaps it is desirable to modify several previously stated alternatives to produce one better alternative.

Present all alternatives for consideration. By considering all ideas as initially feasible, they can be brought out into the open. Such occasions are often called brain storming sessions. Regardless of how silly an idea might seem at first, perhaps when it is considered in the light of other possibilities it may turn out to be a fairly useable solution; or maybe a portion of that idea might be able to be combined with another idea and thereby produce the ultimate solution.

What, for example, would have happened if someone stifled the idea of the paper clip? "Isn't that stupid, who'd want to hold pieces of paper together with bent up wire?" Evidently, people laughed at Columbus, and his idea of a round world; they laughed at John Fulton and his steamship; and even at a young man named Fosbury, who high-jumped backwards. Regardless of ridicule, however, each of these men, in his solution to the problem at hand, succeeded in his particular project.

How many people have been shot-down in creative projects, by comments such as these: "We've tried it and it didn't work," "That's against policy," "It would cost too much," "He hasn't got the experience," "He"'s too young."

List the Alternatives. Looking at the positive side of the argument, there should be positive consideration of all methods, objects, and persons available, to satisfy the needs of decision-making. Once again, write down all of the alternatives, so that they can be comprehensively considered.

To do this, one can list all of the alternatives across the top of a chart and then systematically consider all the factors under each alternative. This chart, or *matrix,* as it is called, can then be used to evaluate the best solution.

As an example, let us assume legislation is passed in each state to award home and business loans and educational benefits to veterans of the Vietnam war. Then a matrix somewhat like this can be made:

	ALTERNATIVES				
	#1	#2	#3	#4	#5
Staff involved					
Labor costs					
Material costs					
Equipment costs					
Services included					
Services excluded					
facilities needed					
Number of veterans processed per day					
Publicity requirements					
Applicable policy					
New policies needed, etc.					

The list can be long, but it is well worth it. If, for example, one is considering attending a community college or university, but can't make up his mind. He can develop a chart with all of the things that are important to him on the side of the chart, and the schools under consideration acros the top. Then a five-point scale can *be* applied to each item, with five being the highest mark and zero the lowest. The school with the most points might be the most likely alternative under all the prevailing circumstances. Still, one cannot be completely definite on this basis alone, so it is necessary to move to the next step in the decision-making process, that of selection.

F. Selecting the Best Alternative Solution. The most important part of the decision-making process is the selection of the most appropriate alternative: *deciding.* This is the stage during which criticism is appropriate. Judgment must be made on all facets of the problem and the alternative solutions. The effectiveness of each of the solutions must be evaluated in terms of the objectives towards which the decision-maker is oriented. He must look carefully at, and criticize severely, such items as cost, timeliness, workability, acceptability, and implementation.

- Can the solution be made to work?
- Will the staff cooperate?
- Will those who are served make the necessary adjustments?
- Are there the skills in the organization to carry out the program?

List the Consequences of the Decision. As these and other items are considered, it is desirable to write down <u>all</u> of the consequences of <u>each</u> of the decisions. List the pro's and con's. It is not enough to add them together and make a decision on that basis, such as in the selection of a college, in the previous section. Not only does one use some type of scale, but he assigns different weights to different items. Using the previous college selection chart, the decision-maker might have to weight costs higher than the availability of co-educational dormitories, or the scholastic reputation of the school over the strength of its football team.

Be a Devil's Advocate. The more desirable alternatives should be scrutinized in a negative way. Take the opposite position, that is, play the *devil's advocate*. Mentally implement the plan and consider the adverse consequences.

Take one of the most favorable-looking alternatives. Ask:

- "Will it affect other departments?"
- "What could go wrong?"
- "What are the potential sources of breakdown?"
- "What new problem might it create?"
- "Where would the resistance be?"

Consider the extent to which these consequences will probably come about and the degree of seriousness of each one. Select second and even third choices in order to plan for contingencies.

Scrutinize the Final Alternative Thoroughly. Once the alternatives have been narrowed to only one, which appears to fill the need, then this one alternative should be subjected to one final round of positive questions:

- Will this decision fulfill the original goal?
- Can the agency live with the decision permanently?
- Is the timing of the decision right?
- Does the decision bring about the greatest benefit for the greatest number?

Involve Your Superiors. It is often necessary and desirable to go to the superiors with the decision. Ordinarily, the problem would be presented, with the attendant factors affecting it, and the alternative solutions which could resolve it. Then the decision-maker would indicate his reasons, with their consequences, for selection of the particular alternative.

G. Implement the Decision. After a decision is made, it must be implemented. The necessary steps must be initiated to carry it out. The whole management cycle of planning, organizing, and controlling must be brought into action, as well as other available management tools.

3. SUMMATION

No phase of the management cycle or any other organizational function could be carried out if decisions were not made. Planning, organizing, controlling, as well as motivating, communicating, and setting standards; these all require endless strings of decisions or choices. This is why the final process of decision making is so important.

Good decisions are the result of understanding responsibilities, involving others, knowing the organization, understanding one's own strengths and weaknesses, and being accountable for decisions made.

In understanding the responsibilities involved, one must know where to get information and be cognizant of the extent to which people can take action.

Through involving others, they gain a sense of ownership in the decision, and become more committed. They remove their defense mechanisms.

Knowing an organization requires an awareness of its organizational history and objectives, where the power centers lie, the limits of one's authority, and the way in which work is actually accomplished.

One's understanding of himself and his own shortcomings insures that he will seek out expertise he does not possess himself, and will develop ways to improve his own skills.

The individual should have this motto: *Remember, when you get right down to it, one person may have to decide – YOU!*

STUDENT LEARNING ACTIVITIES

- Prepare a definition of *decision making,*

- Write a brief paper on the decision-making formula.

- Participate in a class discussion about decision making in a selected public-service agency. Try to identify top, middle, and low-level decisions.

- Prepare a definition of the term *problem*.

- Interview a public-service official to identify a problem within his organization. Follow with a class discussion.

- Prepare a brief paper describing three examples of symptoms and their causes.

- Participate in a problem-solving case study.

- Write a brief paper on why facts must be gathered to aid in the decision-making process.

- Identify the kinds of facts and resources you must use to prepare for making decisions about a teacher-assigned topic.

- Participate in a discussion about fact finding.

- Develop with the class, and have at least 20 students complete, a survey questionnaire with open-ended questions on ways in which your school can be improved. Organize responses according to subject and year ranking of importance.

- Participate in a class discussion on the results of the questionnaire survey.

- After the class has decided on one or more ways in which the school can be improved, prepare a report on one of the objectives including:

    statement of an objective,

    facts needed and how obtained,

    categorizing the facts.

- Deliver an oral version of your report. Respond to questions and comments from the class,

- Choose five articles from the newspaper on five different topics: sports, politics, crime, etc. State the actual problem being addressed.

15

- Participate in a class discussion about problem identification, and problem statements. Sharpen your problem statements if necessary.

- Participate in a class discussion about problems identified and possible alternative solutions.

- Using the example of the State legislature passing a bill awarding home and business loans and educational benefits to veterans of the Gulf War, develop a set of alternative plans as to how the legislation may be carried out.

TEACHER MANAGEMENT ACTIVITIES

- Have students define *decision making*.

- Assign students a paper on the decision-making formula.

- Conduct a class discussion about decision-making in a selected public service agency.

- Have students prepare their own definitions of the term *problem*.

- Assign students interviews with public-service officials to identify selected organizational problems.

- Conduct a class discussion on problems in public-service organizations.

- Have students develop and discuss reports and three examples of symptoms and their causes.

- Select and assign a case study to the class in problem solving.

- Assign a paper on why facts must be gathered to aid in the decision-making process.

- Prepare a list of considerations in several public-service agencies. Have each student select one consideration around which he will gather essential facts to make a decision.

- Conduct a discussion on fact finding.

- Assign the class a survey project, entitled "How Can Our School be Improved?" Have students develop their own questionnaire and administer it to at least 20 students. Ask them to organize their results according to subject and rank of importance.

- Organize a class discussion on the results of the surveys.

- Once one or more items of possible school improvement have been agreed upon, assign the students a report to contain the following:

statement of an objective,

facts needed and how obtained,

categorizing of facts.

- Organize oral presentations of student reports.

- Assign students the reading of five articles from a newspaper on five different topics: sports, polttfcs, crime, etc. Have them state the actual problem being discussed.

- Conduct a class discussion on problem identification and problem statements.

- Assign a brief paper on the symptoms of five problems and the causes in a public service agency selected by each student.

- Conduct a class discussion on the problems and solutions identified.

- Using the example of the new bill for veterans of the Gulf War, have students develop a set of alternatives.

- Insure that the students are open to new and abstract suggestions.

- Direct oral presentations of students in which they review their original problems, the sources and categories of facts, the alternatives available for solution, their respective consequences, and their ultimate decisions. Have students challenge one another's decisions.

Evaluation Questions
Techniques of Decision Making

Read the problem carefully, and answer each of the following questions.

You are a library assistant. Mrs. Smith, the librarian, has two high school aides, Susan and Mary. Mrs. Smith has told you that she may fire Susan if her attitude does not improve. She complained about Susan's laziness and stated that Susan's work was never finished. Mrs. Smith asked you to talk to Susan about improving her attitude. When you tried to talk to Susan about this, she got upset and went home.

After observing the aides' workload for a few days, you notice that Susan has much more work than Mary.

1. What is the problem? _____

2. Name one solution. _____

3. What are the consequences of this solution? _____

4. List another solution. _____

5. What are the consequences of this solution? _____

6. Which do you think is the best solution? _____

18

Read the problem carefully, and answer each of the following questions.

You are in charge of the recreation program at the community center. Your job is to keep activities running smoothly. On the daily schedule, one-half hour has been set aside for basketball. While you have stepped out for a moment, ten of the Green Hornets and ten of the Purple Dragons arrived to play basketball. As each group has two teams set up, neither group would give in. Unfortunately, a fight began. The fight ended just as you returned. Each group plans to play tomorrow. You must make a decision.

1. What is the problem? _____
_____
_____
_____

2. Name one solution. _____
_____
_____
_____

3. What are the consequences of this solution? _____
_____
_____
_____

4. List another solution. _____
_____
_____
_____

5. What are the consequences of this solution? _____
_____
_____
_____

6. Which do you think is the best solution? _____
_____
_____
_____

Answer Key

Answers will vary on this test. The instructor may wish to have a discussion after the test, with students justifying their selections. Students may be evaluated on the soundness of their judgement.

PRINCIPLES AND PRACTICES, OF ADMINISTRATION, SUPERVISION AND MANAGEMENT

TABLE OF CONTENTS

	Page
GENERAL ADMINISTRATION	1
SEVEN BASIC FUNCTIONS OF THE SUPERVISOR	2
I. Planning	2
II. Organizing	3
III. Staffing	3
IV. Directing	3
V. Coordinating	3
VI. Reporting	3
VII. Budgeting	3
PLANNING TO MEET MANAGEMENT GOALS	4
I. What is Planning	4
II. Who Should Make Plans	4
III. What are the Results of Poor Planning	4
IV. Principles of Planning	4
MANAGEMENT PRINCIPLES	5
I. Management	5
II. Management Principles	5
III. Organization Structure	6
ORGANIZATION	8
I. Unity of Command	8
II. Span of Control	8
III. Uniformity of Assignment	9
IV. Assignment of Responsibility and Delegation of Authority	9
PRINCIPLES OF ORGANIZATION	9
I. Definition	9
II. Purpose of Organization	9
III. Basic Considerations in Organizational Planning	9
IV. Bases for Organization	10
V. Assignment of Functions	10
VI. Delegation of Authority and Responsibility	10
VII. Employee Relationships	11

DELEGATING		11
I.	WHAT IS DELEGATING:	11
II.	TO WHOM TO DELEGATE	11
REPORTS		12
I.	DEFINITION	12
II.	PURPOSE	12
III.	TYPES	12
IV.	FACTORS TO CONSIDER BEFORE WRITING REPORT	12
V.	PREPARATORY STEPS	12
VI.	OUTLINE FOR A RECOMMENDATION REPORT	12
MANAGEMENT CONTROLS		13
I.	Control	13
II.	Basis for Control	13
III.	Policy	13
IV.	Procedure	14
V.	Basis of Control	14
FRAMEWORK OF MANAGEMENT		14
I.	Elements	14
II.	Manager's Responsibility	15
III.	Control Techniques	16
IV.	Where Forecasts Fit	16
PROBLEM SOLVING		16
I.	Identify the Problem	16
II.	Gather Data	17
III.	List Possible Solutions	17
IV.	Test Possible Solutions	18
V.	Select the Best Solution	18
VI.	Put the Solution into Actual Practice	19
COMMUNICATION		19
I.	What is Communication?	19
II.	Why is Communication Needed?	19
III.	How is Communication Achieved?	20
IV.	Why Does Communication Fail?	21
V.	How to Improve Communication	21
VI.	How to Determine If You Are Getting Across	21
VII.	The Key Attitude	22
HOW ORDERS AND INSTRUCTIONS SHOULD BE GIVEN		22
I.	Characteristics of Good Orders and Instructions	22
FUNCTIONS OF A DEPARTMENT PERSONNEL OFFICE		23

SUPERVISION
- I. Leadership
  - A. The Authoritarian Approach
  - B. The Laissez-Faire Approach
  - C. The Democratic Approach
- II. Nine Points of Contrast Between Boss and Leader

EMPLOYEE MORALE
- I. Some Ways to Develop and Maintain Good Employee Morale
- II. Some Indicators of Good Morale

MOTIVATION

EMPLOYEE PARTICIPATION
- I. WHAT IS PARTICIPATION
- II. WHY IS IT IMPORTANT?
- III. HOW MAY SUPERVISORS OBTAIN IT?

STEPS IN HANDLING A GRIEVANCE

DISCIPLINE
- I. THE DISCIPLINARY INTERVIEW
- II. PLANNING THE INTERVIEW
- III. CONDUCTING THE INTERVIEW

PRINCIPLES AND PRACTICES, OF
ADMINISTRATION, SUPERVISION AND MANAGEMENT

Most people are inclined to think of administration as something that only a few persons are responsible for in a large organization. Perhaps this is true if you are thinking of Administration with a capital A, but administration with a lower case *a* is a responsibility of supervisors at all levels each working day.

All of us feel we are pretty good supervisors and that we do a good job of administering the workings of our agency. By and large, this is true, but every so often it is good to check up on ourselves. Checklists appear from time to time in various publications which psychologists say tell whether or not a person will make a good wife, husband, doctor, lawyer, or supervisor.

The following questions are an excellent checklist to test yourself as a supervisor and administrator.

Remember, Administration gives direction and points the way but administration carries the ideas to fruition. Each is dependent on the other for its success. Remember, too, that no unit is too small for these departmental functions to be carried out. These statements apply equally as well to the Chief Librarian as to the Department Head with but one or two persons to supervise.

GENERAL ADMINISTRATION: General Responsibilities of Supervisors

1. Have I prepared written statements of functions, activities, and duties for my organizational unit?

2. Have I prepared procedural guides for operating activities?

3. Have I established clearly in writing, lines of authority and responsibility for my organizational unit?

4. Do I make recommendations for improvements in organization, policies, administrative and operating routines and procedures, including simplification of work and elimination of non-essential operations?

5. Have I designated and trained an understudy to function in my absence?

6. Do I supervise and train personnel within the unit to effectively perform their assignments?

7. Do I assign personnel and distribute work on such a basis as to carry out the organizational unit's assignment or mission in the most effective and efficient manner?

8. Have I established administrative controls by:

    a. Fixing responsibility and accountability on all supervisors under my direction for the proper performance of their functions and duties.

b. Preparations and submitting periodic work load and progress reports covering the operations of the unit to my immediate superior.

c. Analysis and evaluation of such reports received from subordinate units.

d. Submission of significant developments and problems arising within the organizational unit to my immediate superior.

e. Conducting conferences, inspections, etc., as to the status and efficiency of unit operations.

9. Do I maintain an adequate and competent working force?

10. Have I fostered good employee-department relations, seeing that established rules, regulations, and instructions are being carried out properly?

11. Do I collaborate and consult with other organizational units performing related functions to insure harmonious and efficient working relationships?

12. Do I maintain liaison through prescribed channels with city departments and other governmental agencies concerned with the activities of the unit?

13. Do I maintain contact with and keep abreast of the latest developments and techniques of administration (professional societies, groups, periodicals, etc.) as to their applicability to the activities of the unit?

14. Do I communicate with superiors and subordinates through prescribed organizational channels?

15. Do I notify superiors and subordinates in instances where bypassing is necessary as soon thereafter as practicable?

16. Do I keep my superior informed of significant developments and problems?

SEVEN BASIC FUNCTIONS OF THE SUPERVISOR

I. PLANNING
This means working out goals and means to obtain goals. <u>What</u> needs to be done, <u>who</u> will do it, <u>how</u>, <u>when</u>, and <u>where</u> it is to be done.

SEVEN STEPS IN PLANNING

A. Define job or problem clearly.
B. Consider priority of job.
C. Consider time-limit—starting and completing.
D. Consider minimum distraction to, or interference with, other activities.
E. Consider and provide for contingencies—possible emergencies.
F. Break job down into components.

G. Consider the 5 W's and H:
    WHY………is it necessary to do the job? (Is the purpose clearly defined?)
    WHAT……..needs to be done to accomplish the defined purpose?
    ………is needed to do the job? (Money, materials, etc.)
    WHO……….is needed to do the job?
    ……….will have responsibilities?
    WHERE……is the work to be done?
    WHEN……..is the job to begin and end? (Schedules, etc.)
    HOW……….is the job to bed done? (Methods, controls, records, etc.)

II. ORGANIZING

This means dividing up the work, establishing clear lines of responsibility and authority and coordinating efforts to get the job done.

III. STAFFING

The whole personnel function of bringing in and <u>training</u> staff, getting the right man and fitting him to the right job—the job to which he is best suited.

In the normal situation, the supervisor's responsibility regarding staffing normally includes providing accurate job descriptions, that is, duties of the jobs, requirements, education and experience, skills, physical, etc.; assigning the work for maximum use of skills; and proper utilization of the probationary period to weed out unsatisfactory employees.

IV. DIRECTING

Providing the necessary leadership to the group supervised. Important work gets done to the supervisor's satisfaction.

V. COORDINATING

The all-important duty of inter-relating the various parts of the work.
The supervisor is also responsible for controlling the coordinated activities. This means measuring performance according to a time schedule and setting quotas to see that the goals previously set are being reached. Reports from workers should be analyzed, evaluated, and made part of all future plans.

VI. REPORTING

This means proper and effective communication to your superiors, subordinates, and your peers (in definition of the job of the supervisor). Reports should be read and information contained therein should be used, not be filed away and forgotten. Reports should be written in such a way that the desired action recommended by the report is forthcoming.

VII. BUDGETING
This means controlling current costs and forecasting future costs. This forecast is based on past experience, future plans and programs, as well as current costs.

You will note that these seven functions can fall under three topics:

- Planning) Make a plan
- Organizing)
- Staffing)
- Directing) Get things done
- Controlling)
- Reporting) Watch it work
- Budgeting)

PLANNING TO MEET MANAGEMENT GOALS

I. **WHAT IS PLANNING?**

   A. Thinking a job through before new work is done to determine the best way to do it
   B. A method of doing something
   C. Ways and means for achieving set goals
   D. A means of enabling a supervisor to deliver with a minimum of effort, all details involved in coordinating his work

II. **WHO SHOULD MAKE PLANS?**

   Everybody!
   All levels of supervision must plan work. (Top management, heads of divisions or bureaus, first line supervisors, and individual employees.) The higher the level, the more planning required.

III. **WHAT ARE THE RESULTS OF POOR PLANNING?**

   A. Failure to meet deadline
   B. Low employee morale
   C. Lack of job coordination
   D. Overtime is frequently necessary
   E. Excessive cost, waste of material and manhours

IV. **PRINCIPLES OF PLANNING**

   A. Getting a clear picture of your objectives. What exactly are you trying to accomplish?
   B. Plan the whole job, then the parts, in proper sequence.
   C. Delegate the planning of details to those responsible for executing them.
   D. Make your plan flexible.
   E. Coordinate your plan with the plans of others so that the work may be processed with a minimum of delay.
   F. Sell your plan before you execute it.
   G. Sell your plan to your superior, subordinate, in order to gain maximum participation and coordination.
   H. Your plan should take precedence. Use knowledge and skills that others have brought to a similar job.
   I. Your plan should take account of future contingencies; allow for future expansion.
   J. Plans should include minor details. Leave nothing to chance that can be anticipated.
   K. Your plan should be simple and provide standards and controls. Establish quality and quantity standards and set a standard method of doing the job. The controls will indicate whether the job is proceeding according to plan.
   L. Consider possible bottlenecks, breakdowns, or other difficulties that are likely to arise.

V. Q. WHAT ARE THE YARDSTICKS BY WHICH PLANNING SHOULD BE MEASURED?
    A. Any plan should:
       — Clearly state a definite course of action to be followed and goal to be achieved, with consideration for emergencies.
       — Be realistic and practical.
       — State what's to be done, when it's to be done, where, how, and by whom.
       — Establish the most efficient sequence of operating steps so that more is accomplished in less time, with the least effort, and with the best quality results.
       — Assure meeting deliveries without delays.
       — Establish the standard by which performance is to be judged.

    Q. WHAT KINDS OF PLANS DOES EFFECTIVE SUPERVISION REQUIRE?
    A. Plans should cover such factors as:
       — Manpower: right number of properly trained employees on the job
       — Materials: adequate supply of the right materials and supplies
       — Machines: full utilization of machines and equipment, with proper maintenance
       — Methods: most efficient handling of operations
       — Deliveries: making deliveries on time
       — Tools: sufficient well-conditioned tools
       — Layout: most effective use of space
       — Reports: maintaining proper records and reports
       — Supervision: planning work for employees and organizing supervisor's own time

MANAGEMENT PRINCIPLES

I. MANAGEMENT
    Q. What do we mean by management?
    A. Getting work done through others.

Management could also be defined as planning, directing, and controlling the operations of a bureau or division so that all factors will function properly and all persons cooperate efficiently for a common objective.

II. MANAGEMENT PRINCIPLES

    A. There should be a hierarchy—wherein authority and responsibility run upward and downward through several levels—with a broad base at the bottom and a single head at the top.

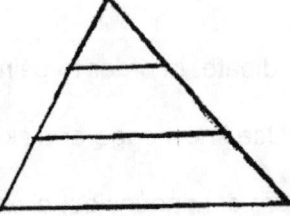

    B. Each and every unit or person in the organization should be answerable ultimately to the manager at the apex. In other words, *The buck stops here!*

C. Every necessary function involved in the bureau's objectives is assigned to a unit in that bureau.

D. Responsibilities assigned to a unit are specifically clear-cut and understood.

E. Consistent methods of organizational structure should be applied at each level of the organization.

F. Each member of the bureau from top to bottom knows: to whom he reports and who reports to him.

G. No member of one bureau reports to more than one supervisor. No dual functions.

H. Responsibility for a function is matched by authority necessary to perform that function. Weight of authority.

I. Individuals or units reporting to a supervisor do not exceed the number which can be feasibly and effectively coordinated and directed. Concept of *span of control*.

J. Channels of command (management) are not violated by staff units, although there should be staff services to facilitate and coordinate management functions.

K. Authority and responsibility should be decentralized to units and individuals who are responsible for the actual performance of operations.
Welfare – down to Welfare Centers
Hospitals – down to local hospitals

L. Management should exercise control through attention to policy problems of exceptional performance, rather than through review of routine actions of subordinates.

M. Organizations should never be permitted to grow so elaborate as to hinder work accomplishments.

III. ORGANIZATION STRUCTURE

Types of Organizations
The purest form is a leader and a few followers, such as:

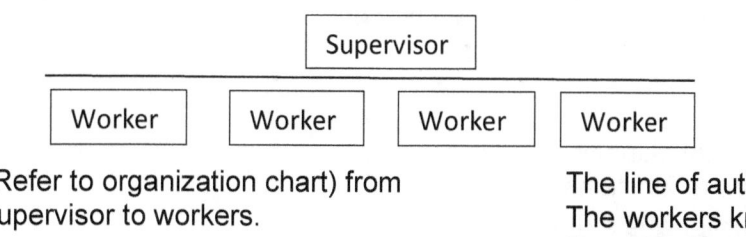

(Refer to organization chart) from supervisor to workers.

The line of authority is direct, The workers know exactly where they stand in relation to their boss, to whom they report for instructions and direction.

Unfortunately, in our present complex society, few organizations are similar to this example of a pure line organization. In this era of specialization, other people are often needed in the simplest of organizations. These specialists are known as staff. The sole purpose for their existence (staff) is to assist, advise, suggest, help or counsel line organizations. Staff has no authority to direct line people—nor do they give them direct instructions.

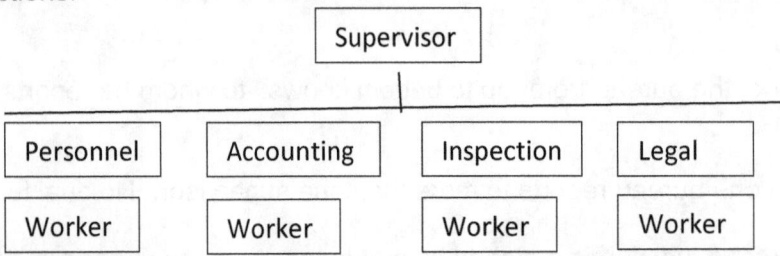

Line Functions
1. Directs
2. Orders
3. Responsibility for carrying out activities from beginning to end
4. Follows chain of command
5. Is identified with what it does
6. Decides when and how to use staff advice
7. Line executes

Staff Functions
1. Advises
2. Persuades and sells
3. Staff studies, reports, recommends but does not carry out
4. May advise across department lines
5. May find its ideas identified with others
6. Has to persuade line to want its advice
7. Staff: Conducts studies and research. Provides advice and instructions in technical matters. Serves as technical specialist to render specific services.

Types and Functions of Organization Charts
An organization chart is a picture of the arrangement and inter-relationship of the subdivisions of an organization.

A. Types of Charts:
   1. Structural: basic relationships only
   2. Functional: includes functions or duties
   3. Personnel: positions, salaries, status, etc.
   4. Process Chart: work performed
   5. Gantt Chart: actual performance against planned
   5. Flow Chart: flow and distribution of work

B. Functions of Charts:
   1. Assist in management planning and control
   2. Indicate duplication of functions
   3. Indicate incorrect stressing of functions
   4. Indicate neglect of important functions
   5. Correct unclear authority
   6. Establish proper span of control

C. Limitations of Charts:
   1. Seldom maintained on current basis
   2. Chart is oversimplified
   3. Human factors cannot adequately be charted

D. Organization Charts should be:
   1. Simple
   2. Symmetrical
   3. Indicate authority
   4. Line and staff relationship differentiated
   5. Chart should be dated and bear signature of approving officer
   6. Chart should be displayed, not hidden

ORGANIZATION

There are four basic principles of organization:
1. Unity of command
2. Span of control
3. Uniformity of assignment
4. Assignment of responsibility and delegation of authority

I. UNITY OF COMMAND

Unity of command means that each person in the organization should receive orders from one, and only one, supervisor. When a person has to take orders from two or more people, (a) the orders may be in conflict and the employee is upset because he does not know which he should obey, or (b) different orders may reach him at the same time and he does not know which he should carry out first.

Equally as bad as having two bosses is the situation where the supervisor is bypassed. Let us suppose you are a supervisor whose boss bypasses you (deals directly with people reporting to you). To the worker, it is the same as having two bosses; but to you, the supervisor, it is equally serious. Bypassing on the part of your boss will undermine your authority, and the people under you will begin looking to your boss for decisions and even for routine orders.

You can prevent bypassing by telling the people you supervise that if anyone tries to give them orders, they should direct that person to you.

II. SPAN OF CONTROL

Span of control on a given level involves:
A. The number of people being supervised
B. The distance
C. The time involved in supervising the people. (One supervisor cannot supervise too many workers effectively.)

Span of control means that a supervisor has the right number (not too many and not too few) of subordinates that he can supervise well.

III. UNIFORMITY OF ASSIGNMENT

In assigning work, you as the supervisor should assign to each person jobs that are similar in nature. An employee who is assigned too many different types of jobs will waste time in going from one kind of work to another. It takes time for him to get to top production in one kind of task and, before he does so, he has to start on another.
When you assign work to people, remember that:

A. Job duties should be definite. Make it clear from the beginning what they are to do, how they are to do it, and why they are to do it. Let them know how much they are expected to do and how well they are expected to do it.
B. Check your assignments to be certain that there are no workers with too many unrelated duties, and that no two people have been given overlapping responsibilities. Your aim should be to have every task assigned to a specific person with the work fairly distributed and with each person doing his part.

IV. ASSIGNMENT OF RESPONSIBILITY AND DELEGATION OF AUTHORITY

A supervisor cannot delegate his final responsibility for the work of his department. The experienced supervisor knows that he gets his work done through people. He can't do it all himself. So he must assign the work and the responsibility for the work to his employees. Then they must be given the authority to carry out their responsibilities.

By assigning responsibility and delegating authority to carry out the responsibility, the supervisor builds in his workers initiative, resourcefulness, enthusiasm, and interest in their work. He is treating them as responsible adults. They can find satisfaction in their work, and they will respect the supervisor and be loyal to the supervisor.

PRINCIPLES OF ORGANIZATION

I. DEFINITION

Organization is the method of dividing up the work to provide the best channels for coordinated effort to get the agency's mission accomplished.

II. PURPOSE OF ORGANIZATION

A. To enable each employee within the organization to clearly know his responsibilities and relationships to his fellow employees and to organizational units
B. To avoid conflicts of authority and overlapping of jurisdiction.
C. To ensure teamwork.

III. BASIC CONSIDERATIONS IIN ORGANIZATIONAL PLANNING

A. The basic plans and objectives of the agency should be determined, and the organizational structure should be adapted to carry out effectively such plans and objectives.
B. The organization should be built around the major functions of the agency and not individuals or groups of individuals.

C. The organization should be sufficiently flexible to meet new and changing conditions which may be brought about from within or outside the department.
D. The organizational structure should be as simple as possible and the number of organizational units kept at a minimum.
E. The number of levels of authority should be kept at a minimum. Each additional management level lengthens the chain of authority and responsibility and increases the time for instructions to be distributed to operating levels and for decisions to be obtained from higher authority.
F. The form of organization should permit each executive to exercise maximum initiative within the limits of delegated authority.

IV. BASES FOR ORGANIZATION

A. Purpose (Examples: education, police, sanitation)
B. Process (Examples: accounting, legal, purchasing)
C. Clientele (Examples: welfare, parks, veteran)
D. Geographic (Examples: borough offices, precincts, libraries)

V. ASSIGNMENTS OF FUNCTIONS

A. Every function of the agency should be assigned to a specific organizational unit. Under normal circumstances, no single function should be assigned to more than one organizational unit.
B. There should be no overlapping, duplication, or conflict between organizational elements.
C. Line functions should be separated from staff functions, and proper emphasis should be placed on staff activities.
D. Functions which are closely related or similar should normally be assigned to a single organizational unit.
E. Functions should be properly distributed to promote balance, and to avoid overemphasis of less important functions and underemphasis of more essential functions.

VI. DELEGATION OF AUTHORITY AND RESPONSIBILITY

A. Responsibilities assigned to a specific individual or organizational unit should carry corresponding authority, and all statements of authority or limitations thereof should be as specific as possible.
B. Authority and responsibility for action should be decentralized to organizational units and individuals responsible for actual performance to the greatest extent possible, without relaxing necessary control over policy or the standardization of procedures. Delegation of authority will be consistent with decentralization of responsibility but such delegation will not divest an executive in higher authority of his overall responsibility.
C. The heads of organizational units should concern themselves with important matters and should delegate to the maximum extent details and routines performed in the ordinary course of business.
D. All responsibilities, authorities, and relationships should be stated in simple language to avoid misinterpretation.
E. Each individual or organizational unit charged with a specific responsibility will be held responsible for results.

VII. EMPLOYEE RELATIONSHIPS
   A. The employees reporting to one executive should not exceed the number which can be effectively directed and coordinated. The number will depend largely upon the scope and extent of the responsibilities of the subordinates.
   B. No person should report to more than one supervisor. Every supervisor should know who reports to him, and every employee should know to whom he reports. Channels of authority and responsibility should not be violated by staff units.
   C. Relationships between organizational units within the agency and with outside organizations and associations should be clearly stated and thoroughly understood to avoid misunderstanding.

DELEGATING

I. WHAT IS DELEGATING?
Delegating is assigning a job to an employee, giving him the authority to get that job done, and giving him the responsibility for seeing to it that the job is done.

   A. What To Delegate
      1. Routine details
      2. Jobs which may be necessary and take a lot of time, but do not have to be done by the supervisor personally (preparing reports, attending meetings, etc.)
      3. Routine decision-making (making decisions which do not require the supervisor's personal attention)

   B. What Not To Delegate
      1. Job details which are *executive functions* (setting goals, organizing employees into a good team, analyzing results so as to plan for the future)
      2. Disciplinary power (handling grievances, preparing service ratings, reprimands, etc.)
      3. Decision-making which involves large numbers of employees or other bureaus and departments
      4. Final and complete responsibility for the job done by the unit being supervised

   C. Why Delegate?
      1. To strengthen the organization by developing a greater number of skilled employees
      2. To improve the employee's performance by giving him the chance to learn more about the job, handle some responsibility, and become more interested in getting the job done
      3. To improve a supervisor's performance by relieving him of routine jobs and giving him more time for *executive functions* (planning, organizing, controlling, etc.) which cannot be delegated

II. TO WHOM TO DELEGATE
People with abilities not being used. Selection should be based on ability, not on favoritism.

REPORTS

I. **DEFINITION**
A report is an orderly presentation of factual information directed to a specific reader for a specific purpose

II. **PURPOSE**
The general purpose of a report is to bring to the reader useful and factual information about a condition or a problem. Some specific purposes of a report may be:

A. To enable the reader to appraise the efficiency or effectiveness of a person or an operation
B. To provide a basis for establishing standards
C. To reflect the results of expenditures of time, effort, and money
D. To provide a basis for developing or altering programs

III. **TYPES**

A. Information Report: Contains facts arranged in sequence
B. Summary (Examination) Report: Contains facts plus an analysis or discussion of the significance of the facts. Analysis may give advantages and disadvantages or give qualitative and quantitative comparisons
C. Recommendation Report: Contains facts, analysis, and conclusion logically drawn from the facts and analysis, plus a recommendation based upon the facts, analysis, and conclusions

IV. **FACTORS TO CONSIDER BEFORE WRITING REPORT**

A. <u>Why</u> write the report?: The purpose of the report should be clearly defined.
B. <u>Who</u> will read the report?: What level of language should be used? Will the reader understand professional or technical language?
C. <u>What</u> should be said?: What does the reader need or want to know about the subject?
D. <u>How</u> should it be said?: Should the subject be presented tactfully? Convincingly? In a stimulating manner?

V. **PREPARATORY STEPS**

A. Assemble the facts: Find out who, why, what, where, when, and how.
B. Organize the facts: Eliminate unnecessary information
C. Prepare an outline: Check for orderliness, logical sequence
D. Prepare a draft: Check for correctness, clearness, completeness, conciseness, and tone
E. Prepare it in final form: Check for grammar, punctuation, appearance

VI. **OUTLINE FOR A RECOMMENDATION REPORT**

Is the report:
A. Correct in information, grammar, and tone?
B. Clear?
C. Complete?

D. Concise?
E. Timely?
F. Worth its cost?

Will the report accomplish its purpose?

MANAGEMENT CONTROLS

I. CONTROL
What is control? What is controlled? Who controls?

The essence of control is action which adjusts operations to predetermined standards, and its basis is information in the hands of managers. Control is checking to determine whether plans are being observed and suitable progress toward stated objectives is being made, and action is taken, if necessary, to correct deviations.

We have a ready-made model for this concept of control in the automatic systems which are widely used for process control in the chemical land petroleum industries. A process control system works this way. Suppose, for example, it is desired to maintain a constant rate of flow of oil through a pipe at a predetermined or set-point value. A signal, whose strength represents the rate of flow, can be produced in a measuring device and transmitted to a control mechanism. The control mechanism, when it detects any deviation of the actual from the set-point signal, will reposition the value regulating flow rate.

II. BASIS FOR CONTROL

A process control mechanism thus acts to adjust operations to predetermined standards and does so on the basis of information it receives. In a parallel way, information reaching a manager gives him the opportunity for corrective action and is his basis for control. He cannot exercise control without such information, and he cannot do a complete job of managing without controlling.

III. POLICY

What is policy?

Policy is simply a statement of an organization's intention to act in certain ways when specified types of circumstances arise. It represents a general decision, predetermined and expressed as a principle or rule, establishing a normal pattern of conduct for dealing with given types of business events—usually recurrent. A statement is therefore useful in economizing the time of managers and in assisting them to discharge their responsibilities equitably and consistently.

Policy is not a means of control, but policy does generate the need for control.

Adherence to policies is not guaranteed nor can it be taken on faith. It has to be verified. Without verification, there is no basis for control. Policy and procedures, although closely related and interdependent to a certain extent, are not synonymous. A policy may be adopted, for example, to maintain a materials inventory not to exceed one million dollars.

A procedure for inventory control could interpret that policy and convert it into methods for keeping within that limit, with consideration, too, of possible but foreseeable expedient deviation.

IV. PROCEDURE

What is procedure?

A procedure specifically prescribes:
A. What work is to be performed by the various participants
B. Who are the respective participants
C. When and where the various steps in the different processes are to be performed
D. The sequence of operations that will insure uniform handling of recurring transactions
E. The paper that is involved, its origin, transition, and disposition

Necessary appurtenances to a procedure are:
A. Detailed organizational chart
B. Flow charts
C. Exhibits of forms, all presented in close proximity to the text of the procedure

V. BASIS OF CONTROL – INFORMATION IN THE HANDS OF MANAGERS

If the basis of control is information in the hands of managers, then reporting is elevated to a level of very considerable importance.

Types of reporting may include:
A. Special reports and routine reports
B. Written, oral, and graphic reports
C. Staff meetings
D. Conferences
E. Television screens
F. Non-receipt of information, as where management is by exception
G. Any other means whereby information is transmitted to a manager as a basis for control action

FRAMEWORK OF MANAGEMENT

I. ELEMENTS

A. Policy: It has to be verified, controlled.

B. Organization is part of the giving of an assignment. The organizational chart gives to each individual in his title, a first approximation of the nature of his assignment and orients him as being accountable to a certain individual. Organization is not in a true sense a means of control. Control is checking to ascertain whether the assignment is executed as intended and acting on the basis of that information.

C. Budgets perform three functions:
1. They present the objectives, plans, and programs of the organization in financial terms.

2. They report the progress of actual performance against these predetermined objectives, plans, and programs.
3. Like organizational charts, delegations of authority, procedures, and job descriptions, they define the assignments which have flowed from the Chief Executive. Budgets are a means of control in the respect that they report progress of actual performance against the program. They provide information which enables managers to take action directed toward bringing actual results into conformity with the program.

D. Internal Check provides in practice for the principle that the same person should not have responsibility for all phases of a transaction. This makes it clearly an aspect of organization rather than of control. Internal Check is static, or built-in.

E. Plans, Programs, Objectives
People must know what they are trying to do. Objectives fulfill this need. Without them, people may work industriously and yet, working aimlessly, accomplish little. Plans and Programs complement Objectives, since they propose how and according to what time schedule the objectives are to be reached.

F. Delegations of Authority
Among the ways we have for supplementing the titles and lines of authority of an organizational chart are delegations of authority. Delegations of authority clarify the extent of authority of individuals and in that way serve to define assignments. That they are not means of control is apparent from the very fact that wherever there has been a delegation of authority, the need for control increases. This could hardly be expected to happen if delegations of authority were themselves means of control.

II. MANAGER'S RESPONSIBILITY

Control becomes necessary whenever a manager delegates authority to a subordinate because he cannot delegate and then simply sit back and forget4 about it. A manager's accountability to his own superior has not diminished one whit as a result of delegating part of his authority to a subordinate. The manager must exercise control over actions taken under the authority so delegated. That means checking serves as a basis for possible corrective action.

Objectives, plans, programs, organizational charts, and other elements of the managerial system are not fruitfully regarded as either controls or means of control. They are pre-established standards or models of performance to which operations are adjusted by the exercise of management control. These standards or models of performance are dynamic in character for they are constantly altered, modified, or revised. Policies, organizational set-up, procedures, delegations, etc. are constantly altered but, like objectives and plans, they remain in force until they are either abandoned or revised. All of the elements (or standards or models of performance), objectives, plans, and programs, policies, organization, etc. can be regarded as a *framework of management*.

III. CONTROL TECHNIQUES

Examples of control techniques:
A. Compare against established standards
B. Compare with a similar operation
C. Compare with past operations
D. Compare with predictions of accomplishment

IV. WHERE FORECASTS FIT

Control is after-the-fact while forecasts are before. Forecasts and projections are important for setting objectives and formulating plans.

Information for aiming and planning does not have to be before-the-fact. It may be an after-the-fact analysis proving that a certain policy has been impolitic in its effect on the relation of the company or department with customer, employee, taxpayer, or stockholder; or that a certain plan is no longer practical, or that a certain procedure is unworkable.

The prescription here certainly would not be in control (in these cases, control would simply bring operations into conformity with obsolete standards) but the establishment of new standards, a new policy, a new plan, and a new procedure to be controlled too.

Information is, of course, the basis for all communication in addition to furnishing evidence to management of the need for reconstructing the framework of management.

PROBLEM SOLVING

The accepted concept in modern management for problem solving is the utilization of the following steps:

A. Identify the problem
B. Gather data
C. List possible solutions
D. Test possible solutions
E. Select the best solution
F. Put the solution into actual practice

Occasions might arise where you would have to apply the second step of gathering data before completing the first step.

You might also find that it will be necessary to work on several steps at the same time.

I. IDENTIFY THE PROBLEM

Your first step is to define as precisely as possible the problem to be solved. While this may sound easy, it is often the most difficult part of the process.

It has been said of problem solving that you are halfway to the solution when you can write out a clear statement of the problem itself.

Our job now is to get below the surface manifestations of the trouble and pinpoint the problem. This is usually accomplished by a logical analysis, by going from the general to the particular; from the obvious to the not-so-obvious cause.

Let us say that production is behind schedule. WHY? Absenteeism is high. Now, is absenteeism the basic problem to be tackled, or is it merely a symptom of low morale among the workforce? Under these circumstances, you may decide that production is not the problem; the problem is *employee morale*.

In trying to define the problem, remember there is seldom one simple reason why production is lagging, or reports are late, etc.

Analysis usually leads to the discovery that an apparent problem is really made up of several subproblems which must be attacked separately.

Another way is to limit the problem, and thereby ease the task of finding a solution, and concentrate on the elements which are within the scope of your control.

When you have gone this far, write out a tentative statement of the problem to be solved.

II. GATHER DATA

In the second step, you must set out to collect all the information that might have a bearing on the problem. Do not settle for an assumption when reasonable fact and figures are available.

If you merely go through the motions of problem-solving, you will probably shortcut the information-gathering step. Therefore, do not stack the evidence by confining your research to your own preconceived ideas.

As you collect facts, organize them in some form that helps you make sense of them and spot possible relationships between them. For example, plotting cost per unit figures on a graph can be more meaningful than a long column of figures.

Evaluate each item as you go along. Is the source material absolutely, reliable, probably reliable, or not to be trusted.

One of the best methods for gathering data is to go out and look the situation over carefully. Talk to the people on the job who are most affected by this problem.

Always keep in mind that a primary source is usually better than a secondary source of information.

III. LIST POSSIBLE SOLUTIONS

This is the creative thinking step of problem solving. This is a good time to bring into play whatever techniques of group dynamics the agency or bureau might have developed for a joint attack on problems.

Now the important thing for you to do is: Keep an open mind. Let your imagination roam freely over the facts you have collected. Jot down every possible solution that occurs to you. Resist the temptation to evaluate various proposals as you go along. List seemingly absurd ideas along with more plausible ones. The more possibilities you list during this step, the less risk you will run of settling for merely a workable, rather than the best, solution.

Keep studying the data as long as there seems to be any chance of deriving additional ideas, solutions, explanations, or patterns from it.

IV. TEST POSSIBLE SOLUTIONS

Now you begin to evaluate the possible solutions. Take pains to be objective. Up to this point, you have suspended judgment but you might be tempted to select a solution you secretly favored all along and proclaim it as the best of the lot.

The secret of objectivity in this phase is to test the possible solutions separately, measuring each against a common yardstick. To make this yardstick try to enumerate as many specific criteria as you can think of. Criteria are best phrased as questions which you ask of each possible solution. They can be drawn from these general categories:

- Suitability – Will this solution do the job?
  Will it solve the problem completely or partially?
  Is it a permanent or a stopgap solution?

- Feasibility - Will this plan work in actual practice?
  Can we afford this approach?
  How much will it cost?

- Acceptability - Will the boss go along with the changes required in the plan?
  Are we trying to drive a tack with a sledge hammer?

V. SELECT THE BEST SOLUTION

This is the area of executive decision.

Occasionally, one clearly superior solution will stand out at the conclusion of the testing process. But often it is not that simple. You may find that no one solution has come through all the tests with flying colors.

You may also find that a proposal, which flunked miserably on one of the essential tests, racked up a very high score on others.

The best solution frequently will turn out to be a combination.

Try to arrange a marriage that will bring together the strong points of one possible solution with the particular virtues of another. The more skill and imagination that you apply, the greater is the likelihood that you will come out with a solution that is not merely adequate and workable, but is the best possible under the circumstances.

VI. PUT THE SOLUTION INTO ACTUAL PRACTICE

As every executive knows, a plan which works perfectly on paper may develop all sorts of bugs when put into actual practice.

Problem-solving does not stop with selecting the solution which looks best in theory. The next step is to put the chosen solution into action and watch the results. The results may point towards modifications.

If the problem disappears when you put your solution into effect, you know you have the right solution.

If it does not disappear, even after you have adjusted your plan to cover unforeseen difficulties that turned up in practice, work your way back through the problem-solving solutions.

>Would one of them have worked better?
>Did you overlook some vital piece of data which would have given you a different slant on the whole situation? Did you apply all necessary criteria in testing solutions? If no light dawns after this much rechecking, it is a pretty good bet that you defined the problem incorrectly in the first place.

You came up with the wrong solution because you tackled the wrong problem.

Thus, step six may become step one of a new problem-solving cycle.

COMMUNICATION

I. WHAT IS COMMUNICATION?
We communicate through writing, speaking, action, or inaction. In speaking to people face-to-face, there is opportunity to judge reactions and to adjust the message. This makes the supervisory chain one of the most, and in many instances the most, important channels of communication.

In an organization, communication means keeping employees informed about the organization's objectives, policies, problems, and progress. Communication is the free interchange of information, ideas, and desirable attitudes between and among employees and between employees and management.

II. WHY IS COMMUNICATION NEEDED?

   A. People have certain social needs
   B. Good communication is essential in meeting those social needs
   C. While people have similar basic needs, at the same time they differ from each other
   D. Communication must be adapted to these individual differences

An employee cannot do his best work unless he knows why he is doing it. If he has the feeling that he is being kept in the dark about what is going on, his enthusiasm and productivity suffer.

Effective communication is needed in an organization so that employees will understand what the organization is trying to accomplish; and how the work of one unit contributes to or affects the work of other units in the organization and other organizations.

III. HOW IS COMMUNICATION ACHIEVED?

Communication flows downward, upward, sideways.

A. Communication may come from top management down to employees. This is downward communication.

Some means of downward communication are:
1. Training (orientation, job instruction, supervision, public relations, etc.)
2. Conferences
3. Staff meetings
4. Policy statements
5. Bulletins
6. Newsletters
7. Memoranda
8. Circulation of important letters

In downward communication, it is important that employees be informed in advance of changes that will affect them.

B. Communications should also be developed so that the ideas, suggestions, and knowledge of employees will flow upward to top management.

Some means of upward communication are:
1. Personal discussion conferences
2. Committees
3. Memoranda
4. Employees suggestion program
5. Questionnaires to be filled in giving comments and suggestions about proposed actions that will affect field operations.

Upward communication requires that management be willing to listen, to accept, and to make changes when good ideas are present. Upward communication succeeds when there is no fear of punishment for speaking out or lack of interest at the top. Employees will share their knowledge and ideas with management when interest is shown and recognition is given.

C. The advantages of downward communication:
1. It enables the passing down of orders, policies, and plans necessary to the continued operation of the station.
2. By making information available, it diminishes the fears and suspicions which result from misinformation and misunderstanding.
3. It fosters the pride people want to have in their work when they are told of good work.
4. It improves the morale and stature of the individual to be *in the know*.

5. It helps employees to understand, accept, and cooperate with changes when they know about them in advance.

D. The advantages of upward communication:
1. It enables the passing upward of information, attitudes, and feelings.
2. It makes it easier to find out how ready people are to receive downward communication.
3. It reveals the degree to which the downward communication is understood and accepted.
4. It helps to satisfy the basic social needs.
5. It stimulates employees to participate in the operation of their organization.
6. It encourage employees to contribute ideas for improving the efficiency and economy of operations.
7. It helps to solve problem situations before they reach the explosion point.

IV. WHY DOES COMMUNICATION FAIL?

A. The technical difficulties of conveying information clearly
B. The emotional content of communication which prevents complete transmission
C. The fact that there is a difference between what management needs to say, what it wants to day, and what it does say
D. The fact that there is a difference between what employees would like to say, what they think is profitable or safe to say, and what they do say

V. HOW TO IMPROVE COMMUNICATION

As a supervisor, you are a key figure in communication. To improve as a communicator, you should:
A. Know: Knowing your subordinates will help you to recognize and work with individual differences.
B. Like: If you like those who work for you and those for whom you work, this will foster the kind of friendly, warm, work atmosphere that will facilitate communication.
C. Trust: Showing a sincere desire to communicate will help to develop the mutual trust and confidence which are essential to the free flow of communication.
D. Tell: Tell your subordinates and superiors *what's doing*. Tell your subordinates *why* as well as *how*.
E. Listen: By listening, you help others to talk and you create good listeners. Don't forget that listening implies action.
F. Stimulate: Communication has to be stimulated and encouraged. Be receptive to ideas and suggestions and motivate your people so that each member of the team identifies himself with the job at hand.
G. Consult: The most effective way of consulting is to let your people participate, insofar as possible, in developing determinations which affect them or their work.

VI. HOW TO DETERMINE WHETHER YOU ARE GETTING ACROSS

A. Check to see that communication is received and understood
B. Judge this understanding by actions rather than words
C. Adapt or vary communication, when necessary
D. Remember that good communication cannot cure all problems

VII. THE KEY ATTITUDE

Try to see things from the other person's point of view. By doing this, you help to develop the permissive atmosphere and the shared confidence and understanding which are essential to effective two-way communication.

Communication is a two-way process:
A. The basic purpose of any communication is to get action.
B. The only way to get action is through acceptance.
C. In order to get acceptance, communication must be humanly satisfying as well as technically efficient.

HOW ORDERS AND INSTRUCTIONS SHOULD BE GIVEN

I. CHARACTERISTICS OF GOOD ORDERS AND INSTRUCTIONS

   A. Clear
      Orders should be definite as to
      —What is to be done
      —Who is to do it
      —When it is to be done
      —Where it is to be done
      —How it is to be done

   B. Concise
      Avoid wordiness. Orders should be brief and to the point.

   C. Timely
      Instructions and orders should be sent out at the proper time and not too long in advance of expected performance.

   D. Possibility of Performance
      Orders should be feasible:
      1. Investigate before giving orders
      2. Consult those who are to carry out instructions before formulating and issuing them

   E. Properly Directed
      Give the orders to the people concerned. Do not send orders to people who are not concerned. People who continually receive instructions that are not applicable to them get in the habit of neglecting instructions generally.

   F. Reviewed Before Issuance
      Orders should be reviewed before issuance:
      1. Test them by putting yourself in the position of the recipient
      2. If they involve new procedures, have the persons who are to do the work review them for suggestions.

   G. Reviewed After Issuance
      Persons who receive orders should be allowed to raise questions and to point out unforeseen consequences of orders.

H. Coordinated
Orders should be coordinated so that work runs smoothly.

I. Courteous
Make a request rather than a demand. There is no need to continually call attention to the fact that you are the boss.

J. Recognizable as an Order
Be sure that the order is recognizable as such.

K. Complete
Be sure recipient has knowledge and experience sufficient to carry out order. Give illustrations and examples.

A DEPARTMENTAL PERSONNEL OFFICE IS RESPONSIBLE FOR THE FOLLOWING FUNCTIONS

1. Policy
2. Personnel Programs
3. Recruitment and Placement
4. Position Classification
5. Salary and Wage Administration
6. Employee performance Standards and Evaluation
7. Employee Relations
8. Disciplinary Actions and Separations
9. Health and Safety
10. Staff Training and Development
11. Personnel Records, Procedures, and Reports
12. Employee Services
13. Personnel Research

SUPERVISION

I. LEADERSHIP

All leadership is based essentially on authority. This comes from two sources: It is received from higher management or it is earned by the supervisor through his methods of supervision. Although effective leadership has always depended upon the leader's using his authority in such a way as to appeal successfully to the motives of the people supervised, the conditions for making this appeal are continually changing. The key to today's problem of leadership is flexibility and resourcefulness on the part of the leader in meeting changes in conditions as they occur.

Three basic approaches to leadership are generally recognized:

A. The Authoritarian Approach
   1. The methods and techniques used in this approach emphasize the *I* in leadership and depend primarily on the formal authority of the leader. This authority is sometimes exercised in a hardboiled manner and sometimes in a benevolent

manner, but in either case the dominating role of the leader is reflected in the thinking, planning, and decisions of the group.
2. Group results are to a large degree dependent on close supervision by the leader. Usually, the individuals in the group will not show a high degree of initiative or acceptance of responsibility and their capacity to grow and develop probably will not be fully utilized. The group may react with resentment or submission, depending upon the manner and skill of the leader in using his authority.
3. This approach develops as a natural outgrowth of the authority that goes with the leader's job and his feeling of sole responsibility for getting the job done. It is relatively easy to use and does not require must resourcefulness.
4. The use of this approach is effective in times of emergencies, in meeting close deadline as a final resort, in settling some issues, in disciplinary matters, and with dependent individuals and groups.

B. The Laissez-Faire or Let 'em Alone Approach
1. This approach generally is characterized by an avoidance of leadership responsibility by the leader. The activities of the group depend largely on the choice of its members rather than the leader.
2. Group results probably will be poor. Generally, there will be disagreements over petty things, bickering, and confusion. Except for a few aggressive people, individuals will not show much initiative and growth and development will be retarded. There may be a tendency for informal leaders to take over leadership of the group.
3. This approach frequently results from the leader's dislike of responsibility, from his lack of confidence, from failure of other methods to work, from disappointment or criticism. It is usually the easiest of the three to use and requires both understanding and resourcefulness on the part of the leader.
4. This approach is occasionally useful and effective, particularly in forcing dependent individuals or groups to rely on themselves, to give someone a chance to save face by clearing his own difficulties, or when action should be delayed temporarily for good cause.

C. The Democratic Approach
1. The methods and techniques used in this approach emphasize the *we* in leadership and build up the responsibility of the group to attain its objectives. Reliance is placed largely on the earned authority of the leader.
2. Group results are likely to be good because most of the job motives of the people will be satisfied. Cooperation and teamwork, initiative, acceptance of responsibility, and the individual's capacity for growth probably will show a high degree of development.
3. This approach grows out of a desire or necessity of the leader to find ways to appeal effectively to the motivation of his group. It is the best approach to build up inside the person a strong desire to cooperate and apply himself to the job. It is the most difficult to develop, and requires both understanding and resourcefulness on the part of the leader.
4. The value of this approach increases over a long period where sustained efficiency and development of people are important. It may not be fully effective in all situations, however, particularly when there is not sufficient time to use it properly or where quick decisions must be made.

All three approaches are used by most leaders and have a place in supervising people. The extent of their use varies with individual leaders, with some using one approach predominantly. The leader who uses these three approaches, and varies their use with time and circumstance, is probably the most effective. Leadership which is used predominantly with a democratic approach requires more resourcefulness on the part of the leader but offers the greatest possibilities in terms of teamwork and cooperation.

The one best way of developing democratic leadership is to provide a real sense of participation on the part of the group, since this satisfies most of the chief job motives. Although there are many ways of providing participation, consulting as frequently as possible with individuals and groups on things that affect them seems to offer the most in building cooperation and responsibility. Consultation takes different forms, but it is most constructive when people feel they are actually helping in finding the answers to the problems on the job.

There are some requirements of leaders in respect to human relations which should be considered in their selection and development. Generally, the leader should be interested in working with other people, emotionally stable, self-confident, and sensitive to the reactions of others. In addition, his viewpoint should be one of getting the job done through people who work cooperatively in response to his leadership. He should have a knowledge of individual and group behavior, but, most important of all, he should work to combine all of these requirements into a definite, practical skill in leadership.

II. NINE POINTS OF CONTRAST BETWEEN *BOSS* AND *LEADER*

   A. The boss drives his men; the leader coaches them.
   B. The boss depends on authority; the leader on good will.
   C. The boss inspires fear; the leader inspires enthusiasm.
   D. The boss says I; the leader says *We*.
   E. The boss says *Get here on time*; the leader gets there ahead of time.
   F. The boss fixes the blame for the breakdown; the leader fixes the breakdown.
   G. The boss knows how it is done; the leader shows how.
   H. The boss makes work a drudgery; the leader makes work a game.
   I. The boss says *Go*; the leader says *Let's go*.

EMPLOYEE MORALE

Employee morale is the way employees feel about each other, the organization or unit in which they work, and the work they perform.

I. SOME WAYS TO DEVELOP AND MAINTAIN GOOD EMPLYEE MORALE

   A. Give adequate credit and praise when due.
   B. Recognize importance of all jobs and equalize load with proper assignments, always giving consideration to personality differences and abilities.
   C. Welcome suggestions and do not have an *all-wise* attitude. Request employees' assistance in solving problems and use assistants when conducting group meetings on certain subjects.
   D. Properly assign responsibilities and give adequate authority for fulfillment of such assignments.

E. Keep employees informed about matters that affect them.
F. Criticize and reprimand employees privately.
G. Be accessible and willing to listen.
H. Be fair.
I. Be alert to detect training possibilities so that you will not miss an opportunity to help each employee do a better job, and if possible with less effort on his part.
J. Set a good example.
K. Apply the golden rule.

II. SOME INDICATIONS OF GOOD MORALE

A. Good quality of work
B. Good quantity
C. Good attitude of employees
D. Good discipline
E. Teamwork
F. Good attendance
G. Employee participation

MOTIVATION

DRIVES

A drive, stated simply, is a desire or force which causes a person to do or say certain things. These are some of the most usual drives and some of their identifying characteristics recognizable in people motivated by such drives:

A. Security (desire to provide for the future)
   Always on time for work
   Works for the same employer for many years
   Never takes unnecessary chances
   Seldom resists doing what he is told

B. Recognition (desire to be rewarded for accomplishment)
   Likes to be asked for his opinion
   Becomes very disturbed when he makes a mistake
   Does things to attract attention
   Likes to see his name in print

C. Position (desire to hold certain status in relation to others)
   Boasts about important people he knows
   Wants to be known as a key man
   Likes titles
   Demands respect
   Belongs to clubs, for prestige

D. Accomplishment (desire to get things done)
   Complains when things are held up
   Likes to do things that have tangible results
   Never lies down on the job
   Is proud of turning out good work

E. Companionship (desire to associate with other people)
   Likes to work with others
   Tells stories and jokes
   Indulges in horseplay
   Finds excuses to talk to others on the job

F. Possession (desire to collect and hoard objects)
   Likes to collect things
   Puts his name on things belonging to him
   Insists on the same location

Supervisors may find that identifying the drives of employees is a helpful step toward motivating them to self-improvement and better job performance. For example: An employee's job performance is below average. His supervisor, having previously determined that the employee is motivated by a drive for security, suggests that taking training courses will help the employee to improve, advance, and earn more money. Since earning more money can be a step toward greater security, the employee's drive for security would motivate him to take the training suggested by the supervisor. In essence, this is the process of charting an employee's future course by using his motivating drives to positive advantage.

EMPLOYEE PARTICIPATION

I. WHAT IS PARTICIPATION

Employee participation is the employee's giving freely of his time, skill, and knowledge to an extent which cannot be obtained by demand.

II. WHY IS IT IMPORTANT?

The supervisor's responsibility is to get the job done through people. A good supervisor gets the job done through people who work willingly and well. The participation of employees is important because:

A. Employees develop a greater sense of responsibility when they share in working out operating plans and goals.
B. Participation provides greater opportunity and stimulation for employees to learn, and to develop their ability.
C. Participation sometimes provides better solutions to problems because such solutions may combine the experience and knowledge of interested employees who want the solutions to work.
D. An employee or group may offer a solution which the supervisor might hesitate to make for fear of demanding too much.

E. Since the group wants to make the solution work, they exert pressure in a constructive way on each other.
F. Participation usually results in reducing the need for close supervision.

II. HOW MAY SUPERVISORS OBTAIN IT?

Participation is encouraged when employees feel that they share some responsibility for the work and that their ideas are sincerely wanted and valued. Some ways of obtaining employee participation are:

A. Conduct orientation programs for new employees to inform them about the organization and their rights and responsibilities as employees.
B. Explain the aims and objectives of the agency. On a continuing basis, be sure that the employees know what these aims and objectives are.
C. Share job successes and responsibilities and give credit for success.
D. Consult with employees, both as individuals and in groups, about things that affect them.
E. Encourage suggestions for job improvements. Help employees to develop good suggestions. The suggestions can bring them recognition. The city's suggestion program offers additional encouragement through cash awards.

The supervisor who encourages employee participation is not surrendering his authority. He must still make decisions and initiate action, and he must continue to be ultimately responsible for the work of those he supervises. But, through employee participation, he is helping his group to develop greater ability and a sense of responsibility while getting the job done faster and better.

STEPS IN HANDLING A GRIEVANCE

1. Get the Facts
    a. Listen sympathetically
    b. Let him talk himself out
    c. Get his story straight
    d. Get his point of view
    e. Don't argue with him
    f. Give him plenty of time
    g. Conduct the interview privately
    h. Don't try to shift the blame or pass the buck

2. Consider the Facts
    a. Consider the employee's viewpoint
    b. How will the decision affect similar cases
    c. Consider each decision as a possible precedent
    d. Avoid snap judgments—don't jump to conclusions

3. Make or Get a Decision
    a. Frame an effective counter-proposal
    b. Make sure it is fair to all
    c. Have confidence in your judgment
    d. Be sure you can substantiate your decision

4. Notify the Employee of Your Decision
   Be sure he is told; try to convince him that the decision is fair and just.

5. Take Action When Needed and If Within Your Authority
   Otherwise, tell employee that the matter will be called to the attention of the proper person or that nothing can be done, and why it cannot.

6. Follow through to see that the desired result is achieved.

7. Record key facts concerning the complaint and the action taken.

8. Leave the way open to him to appeal your decision to a higher authority.

9. Report all grievances to your superior, whether they are appealed or not.

DISCIPLINE

Discipline is training that develops self-control, orderly conduct, and efficiency.

To discipline does not necessarily mean to punish.

To discipline does mean to train, to regulate, and to govern conduct.

I. THE DISCIPLINARY INTERVIEW

Most employees sincerely want to do what is expected of them. In other words, they are self-disciplined. Some employees, however, fail to observe established rules and standards, and disciplinary action by the supervisor is required.

The primary purpose of disciplinary action is to improve conduct without creating dissatisfaction, bitterness, or resentment in the process.

Constructive disciplinary action is more concerned with causes and explanations of breaches of conduct than with punishment. The disciplinary interview is held to get at the causes of apparent misbehavior and to motivate better performance in the future.

It is important that the interview be kept on an impersonal a basis as possible. If the supervisor lets the interview descend to the plane of an argument, it loses its effectiveness.

II. PLANNING THE INTERVIEW

Get all pertinent facts concerning the situation so that you can talk in specific terms to the employee.

Review the employee's record, appraisal ratings, etc.

Consider what you know about the temperament of the employee. Consider your attitude toward the employee. Remember that the primary requisite of disciplinary action is fairness.

Don't enter upon the interview when angry.

Schedule the interview for a place which is private and out of hearing of others.

III. CONDUCTING THE INTERVIEW

   A. Make an effort to establish accord.
   B. Question the employee about the apparent breach of discipline. Be sure that the question is not so worded as to be itself an accusation.
   C. Give the employee a chance to tell his side of the story. Give him ample opportunity to talk.
   D. Use understanding—listening except where it is necessary to ask a question or to point out some details of which the employee may not be aware. If the employee misrepresents facts, make a plain, accurate statement of the facts, but don't argue and don't engage in personal controversy.
   E. Listen and try to understand the reasons for the employee's (mis)conduct. First of all, don't assume that there has been a breach of discipline. Evaluate the employee's reasons for his conduct in the light of his opinions and feelings concerning the consistency and reasonableness of the standards which he was expected to follow. Has the supervisor done his part in explaining the reasons for the rule? Was the employee's behavior unintentional or deliberate? Does he think he had real reasons for his actions? What new facts is he telling? Do the facts justify his actions? What causes, other than those mentioned, could have stimulated the behavior?
   F. After listening to the employee's version of the situation, and if censure of his actions is warranted, the supervisor should proceed with whatever criticism is justified. Emphasis should be placed on future improvement rather than exclusively on the employee's failure to measure up to expected standards of job conduct.
   G. Fit the criticism to the individual. With one employee, a word of correction may be all that is required.
   H. Attempt to distinguish between unintentional error and deliberate misbehavior. An error due to ignorance requires training and not censure.
   I. Administer criticism in a controlled, even tone of voice, never in anger. Make it clear that you are acting as an agent of the department. In general, criticism should refer to the job or the employee's actions and not to the person. Criticism of the employee's work is not an attack on the individual.
   J. Be sure the interview does not destroy the employee's self-confidence. Mention his good qualities and assure him that you feel confident that he can improve his performance.
   K. Wherever possible, before the employee leaves the interview, satisfy him that the incident is closed, that nothing more will be said on the subject unless the offense is repeated.